Teaching the Cause

Ruhi Institute

Books in the Series:

Below are the current titles in the series designed by the Ruhi Institute. The books are intended to be used as the main sequence of courses in a systematic effort to enhance the capacity of youth and adults to serve their communities. The Ruhi Institute is also developing a set of courses that branch out from the third book in the series for training Bahá'í children's classes teachers, and this is indicated in the list as well. It should be noted that the list will undergo change as experience in the field advances, and new titles will be added as an increasing number of curricular elements under development reach the stage where they can be made widely available.

Book 1	*Reflections on the Life of the Spirit*
Book 2	*Arising to Serve*
Book 3	*Teaching Children's Classes Grade 1*
	Teaching Children's Classes Grade 2 (branch course, in pre-publication form)
	Teaching Children's Classes Grade 3 (branch course, in pre-publication form)
Book 4	*The Twin Manifestations*
Book 5	*Releasing the Powers of Junior Youth* (pre-publication edition)
Book 6	*Teaching the Cause*
Book 7	*Walking Together on a Path of Service*
Book 8	*The Covenant of Bahá'u'lláh* (pre-publication edition)

Copyright © 1990 by the Ruhi Foundation, Colombia
All rights reserved. Edition 1.1.1.PE published February 1998
Edition 1.3.1.PE October 2012
ISBN 978-958-98322-8-8

Ruhi Institute
Apartado Postal: 402032
Cali, Colombia
Tel: 57 2 828-2599
Email: instituto@ruhi.org
Web site: www.ruhi.org

Contents

To the Collaborators.................................... 1

The Spiritual Nature of Teaching 5

The Qualities and Attitudes of the Teacher 39

The Act of Teaching.................................... 83

TO THE COLLABORATORS

Book 2 of the Ruhi Institute offered the participants an initial introduction to teaching. The focus was twofold: on learning to visit newly enrolled believers and discuss with them certain deepening themes, and on acquiring the ability to incorporate into one's conversations Bahá'í ideas, drawing upon the language used by 'Abdu'l-Bahá in His talks and Tablets. Having now gained some practical experience, the participants in the program are no doubt eager to embark on a more in-depth exploration of the subject of teaching.

This book consists of three units. The first, "The Spiritual Nature of Teaching", is intended to enhance the participants' understanding of the spiritual significance of teaching. The second, "The Qualities and Attitudes of the Teacher" provides the opportunity to reflect on the attributes that a teacher of the Cause should strive to acquire. In the third unit, "The Act of Teaching", approaches to personal teaching endeavors and collective campaigns are discussed.

Among the various themes treated in the units, two run through the entire book and are explored in various contexts. Those who act as tutors of the course should ensure that the participants acquire a thorough understanding of the ideas involved.

The first of these themes is on "being" and "doing" as two inseparable dimensions of Bahá'í life. It is emphasized that to become effective teachers we must strive daily to refine our inner lives and, at the same time, engage regularly in teaching and gain experience. Unfortunately, in today's world, creating dichotomies is a widespread habit of the mind which can be easily carried over into the Bahá'í community. Should I study or pioneer? Should I attend to the needs of my family or serve the Faith? Should I concentrate on perfecting myself or should I teach others? Accepting this last dichotomy—which is, in the final analysis, imaginary—paralyzes the individual believer, and it is hoped that this course will help its students avoid such paralysis.

The second theme, as important as the first, is about learning. It is maintained that effectiveness in teaching, both individual and collective, can be developed over time, if we approach it in a posture of learning. Experience indicates that the realization of this simple fact and a willingness to adopt the characteristics that define such a posture can open the door to success.

The book moves from the abstract to the practical, focusing attention on the concepts, qualities, attitudes and skills that enhance one's capability to teach. The first unit works largely at the level of concepts: the nature of a duty prescribed unto us by the Manifestation; the commandment to teach as a token of God's bounty; enkindlement; the relation between teaching and knowledge; sacredness; teaching as a sacred duty of every Bahá'í; teaching as the unlocking of the gates to the city of the human heart; teaching as an act that sets in motion a process of spiritual transformation; the Word of God as the power that effects this transformation; and the role of love in teaching.

To say that the first unit largely deals with concepts does not mean that discussion should remain at the level of abstractions. The tutor of the group should see to it that the purpose of the various exercises is indeed accomplished, namely, that understanding is profound enough to affect attitudes and to motivate the participants to equip themselves with the necessary skills and abilities. Particularly, in a world from which the very notion of sacredness is disappearing, in which almost everything is reduced to an act of buying and selling, the students need to emerge from the course with an acute awareness of "the sacred", conscious that, when teaching, they are interacting with the human heart and the myriad spiritual forces that guide a person to recognition and then to certitude.

The second unit explores the spiritual qualities and the attitudes of the teacher. The initial sections are dedicated to reflection on such qualities as purity of heart, selflessness, faith, courage, wisdom, detachment, humility and ardor. The development of spiritual qualities is a theme that is addressed repeatedly in the books of the Ruhi Institute, but in different contexts. Here the purpose is to identify the implications of these attributes for teaching; therefore, the discussion of the group should go beyond generalities and focus on how each quality enhances the teacher's effectiveness.

Attitudes have to do with our responses to situations, and have their roots in our culture, our upbringing, our memories, our past experience and, of course, in our spiritual qualities. Our openness towards people and the sympathy we have for their struggle to understand the truth are examples of attitudes that affect teaching. In this unit the discussion of attitudes in the latter sections is built on the insights gained into spiritual qualities through the study of the first sections. The flow of ideas occurs naturally in the treatment of humility as an essential requisite for a posture of learning. A learning attitude towards teaching, resulting from true humility, lies at the heart of all the attitudes that are praiseworthy in a teacher.

It is hoped that the ideas covered in these sections will convince the students that, in their teaching endeavors, they need to follow a pattern of consultation, action and reflection—to engage regularly in the act of teaching, to reflect on the results of their efforts, to consult with their fellow believers on the effectiveness of what they have said and done, to turn to the writings for answers to the questions that arise, and to modify their methods in the light of experience and the insights gained from the study of the writings. A first fruit of this action and reflection should be an understanding of how the principle of moderation operates in teaching: that the degree of receptivity of each individual determines how he or she should be approached—whether boldly or cautiously, whether directly or indirectly, whether with a challenging or conciliatory tone.

In going through this unit with the group, the tutor must realize that the perfection of spiritual qualities and the conscious change of attitudes do not occur without effort. An important initial step is, of course, to understand the relevant concepts. For example, understanding the concept of generosity and its implications for behavior contributes to the development of this attribute. But, beyond understanding, one must possess the will and the sincere desire to advance spiritually. Will and desire are not created by mere intellectual discussion; there is need for deep and profound reflection by each individual on his or her inner state. It is the task of the tutor, then, to create an environment conducive to such reflection—an environment that does not give rise to feelings of guilt, that does not call for confessions, that does not encourage accusations, one in which a group of friends can dispassionately discuss both abstract and practical matters, leaving each to reflect privately on what is required of him or her.

The third unit focuses on the act of teaching itself. The skills and abilities that a teacher of the Cause must strive to develop are considered in the context of both personal plans and collective projects. Here again, a false dichotomy—the holding of these two facets of teaching in counterposition to each other—can sometimes leave a Bahá'í community paralyzed. The passages presented in this unit and the corresponding exercises are aimed at creating the resolve in the student to become involved in both types of teaching throughout his or her Bahá'í life.

Some crucial concepts which the group is to examine with the assistance of the tutor are: that proclamation is one element of teaching, but alone does not constitute teaching, which entails dialogue between confirmed believers and those willing to investigate the truth of Bahá'u'lláh's claim; that while we should lose no opportunity to proclaim the Faith and teach indirectly, at this point in human history when receptivity is high, we need to acquire and refine the skills and abilities of direct teaching; that our challenge today is to win over to the Cause large numbers, yet enrollment should not be the only outcome sought by our teaching efforts; that teaching does not end when a person enrolls in the community, but should continue until the declarant becomes a confirmed and ardent supporter of the Faith; that for a sustained process of large-scale expansion and consolidation, institute programs are essential in order to develop human resources who will nurture the steadily growing numbers of believers.

In the context of direct teaching, a few sections of the third unit analyze the content of the message to be conveyed to the seeker. This is done with the aid of an example, in this case that of a young person teaching one of her friends. The introduction to the Faith outlined here should not be taken as a formula to be used indiscriminately. What is important for the participants to realize is that their presentation should not consist of a random selection of ideas and principles and that a great deal of thought has to be given to formulating it.

Finally, the participants of the course are asked to devise a personal teaching plan and to participate in at least one national, regional or local campaign. This practical experience is essential if they are to derive full benefit from the study of the book. The tutor will, of course, help them with their efforts in this direction, calling upon the assistance of the relevant institutions—Auxiliary Board members, Assemblies and committees.

The Spiritual Nature of Teaching

Purpose

To understand that teaching is an act of particular spiritual significance. To appreciate that effective teaching involves both "being" and "doing"—attention to one's inner condition as well as constant activity.

SECTION 1

In this unit we will explore the concept of teaching the Cause as an act of particular spiritual significance. In your studies of the writings you have read and discussed passages related to various aspects of teaching, and these, together with your participation in the consultations and activities of the community, have helped you formulate your own ideas on a subject that receives enormous attention from Bahá'ís everywhere. To begin, then, express some of your thoughts about teaching by completing the following sentences:

Teaching is _sharing knowledge_.

Teaching is _Reaching out to other_.

Teaching is _an spiritual act_.

Teaching is _a skill_.

Teaching is _Understing others on a different level_.

SECTION 2

We often hear that "Teaching is the sacred duty of every Bahá'í." What does it mean for teaching to be a duty of the individual believer? The most immediate answer, of course, is that it is a commandment given by Bahá'u'lláh to every one of His followers. **"Teach ye the Cause of God, O people of Bahá,"** is His call, **"for God hath prescribed unto every one the duty of proclaiming His Message, and regardeth it as the most meritorious of all deeds."** [1]

The word "duty" is used in human speech in a number of ways. At times, it carries the notion of a set of rules imposed on us for no apparent reason. We think of certain duties as tasks we must perform even though it would be far more pleasant if we could avoid doing them. Other duties, related to our own well-being and that of those for whom we care, we undertake with relative pleasure. In consultation with your group, make a list of a few enjoyable duties:

In general, we tend to carry out with diligence those duties which seem important to us. A farmer, for example, cares dutifully for his farm because he knows that each task is essential to the final goal of reaping an abundant harvest, upon which the sustenance of his family depends. In the light of your statements on teaching in the previous section, mention some of the fruits that your teaching efforts can yield:

_____
_____
_____
_____
_____
_____
_____
_____
_____

The duties enjoined upon us by the Manifestation of God are conducive to the greatest good. Yet their value does not lie solely in the good they produce. God's commandments and laws are not mere rules telling us what to do or not to do; they are, in essence, statements about the reality of human existence. A simple example will clarify this point.

We know that in order to live a healthy life we need to eat a moderate amount of food on a regular basis. Eating regularly, however, is not an arbitrary rule of behavior someone has imposed on us; it is a statement about the reality of our physical existence. Our bodies are made up in such a way that they require nourishment every so many hours, and we must respond to this requirement; neglecting it will ultimately lead to death.

In the same way, when the Manifestation of God gives us a commandment, for example, one requiring us to pray every day, He is not imposing upon us some arbitrary rule of behavior. His commandment is a statement about the reality of our existence. It tells us that the human soul was created in such a way that we are required to turn our hearts and minds regularly towards God and "converse" with the Source of our being. Likewise, the commandment to teach His Cause, beyond the obvious benefit it brings to us and to humanity, expresses truths about the nature of the human soul and its requirements. In the next few sections we will explore some of these truths. Before doing this, however, you may find it helpful to write a sentence about the nature of each of the following. An example is given to assist you.

1. A candle: The nature of a candle is to give light.

2. A moth: _____

    _____

3. A flame: _is to produce heat_

4. A fountain: _'_

5. Rain clouds: _w_

6. Perfume: _____

Would you agree that the nature of a human being is to give ceaselessly—to give of one's possessions, time, energy and knowledge?

SECTION 3

Let us begin our reflections on some of the implications of the commandment to teach by studying a few quotations from the Writings of 'Abdu'l-Bahá:

> "O servant of God! Rejoice through the glad-tidings of God, be happy by the wafting of the fragrance of God, and cling to the Kingdom of God in such wise that it makes thee separate thyself from the world and kindle in thy heart the fire of the love of God to such an extent that any one who approaches thee will feel its warmth; and if thou desirest to attain to this station, thou shouldst turn thyself wholly unto God. Perhaps an illumination will descend upon thee by which the fragrances of God will be diffused throughout those regions and districts and thou wilt be a lamp of guidance from which the lights of knowledge will emanate and spread in those far countries and distant lands." [2]

According to this passage, we must _Rejoice_ through the glad-tidings of God, _be happy_ by the wafting of the fragrance of God, and _cling_ to the Kingdom of God. This we should do in such wise that we become _separate_ from the world and _kindle_ in our hearts the _fire_ of the _love of God_ so that anyone who approaches us may _feel_ its _warmth_. If we wish to attain this station, we must turn ourselves _wholly unto God_. Then, by the grace of God, we may become lamps of _guidance_ from which the _lights_ of _knowledge_ will _emanate_.

The Spiritual Nature of Teaching - 9

SECTION 4

'Abdu'l-Bahá wrote the following words to one of the friends who, having long desired to attain His presence, finally had a brief meeting with Him:

> "But I hope that this meeting became as the wick of the lamp and the fire—that as soon as it was touched it became ignited. I am expecting the results of this meeting, that I may see thee lighted as a candle and burning thyself as a moth with the fire of the love of God, weeping like unto the cloud by the greatness of love and attraction, laughing like unto the meadow and stirred into cheerfulness like unto the young tree by the wafting of the breeze of the Paradise of Abhá!" [3]

According to the above passage, 'Abdu'l-Bahá would like to see us lighted as ___ _____, burning ourselves as _____, weeping like unto _____ _____, laughing like unto _____, and stirred into cheerfulness like unto _____. We should be burning with the fire of _the love of God_, weeping by the greatness of _____, and stirred into cheerfulness by the wafting of the _____ _____.

SECTION 5

And in a Tablet written in reply to questions from one of the friends, 'Abdu'l-Bahá stated:

> "The handmaids of God must rise to such a station that they will, by themselves and unaided, comprehend these inner meanings, and be able to expound at full length every single word; a station where, out of the truth of their inmost hearts, a spring of wisdom will well up, and jet forth even as a fountain that leapeth from its own original source." [4]

'Abdu'l-Bahá desires that we rise to such a station that we will, by ourselves and unaided, _comprehend_ the inner meanings of the Teachings and be able to _expound_ at full length _every single word_. This is the station where, out of the _truth_ of our inmost hearts, a _____ _____ will well up, and _____ even as a _____ that _____ from its own _____.

SECTION 6

The three quotations from the Writings of 'Abdu'l-Bahá we have studied suggest that the commandment of Bahá'u'lláh to teach His Cause concerns not only the actions we must carry out, but also a state of being we must attain. There is much we can learn about this state of being from the images contained in the quotations. They speak of things whose very existence requires them to give of themselves. Can a flame choose not to give forth light and yet be called a flame? Can a fountain choose not to flow and still be a fountain? So too, we are created to be giving and generous. To give, to share with others what we possess is a requirement of our spiritual existence. Of all that we possess the most precious is the recognition of Bahá'u'lláh as the Manifestation of God for today. It is only natural that we would share with others the knowledge we receive from His Revelation and the love and joy with which this Revelation fills our souls.

There will, of course, be many obstacles in our way as we strive to be teachers of the Cause. We may be shy, we may be fearful to act or to speak forth, we may find it difficult to express our thoughts and our sentiments, but all these we can gradually overcome if we understand that by teaching the Cause of God, we are learning to give freely of that which is most dear to us. The following words from a letter written on behalf of the Guardian can serve as a constant reminder to us of our duty to share with others the Message of Bahá'u'lláh:

> **"The world is in great turmoil, and its problems seem to become daily more acute. We should, therefore, not sit idle, otherwise we would be failing in carrying out our sacred duty. Bahá'u'lláh has not given us His Teachings to treasure them and hide them for our personal delight and pleasure. He gave them to us that we may pass them from mouth to mouth, until all the world becomes familiar with them, and enjoys their blessings and uplifting influence."** [5]

SECTION 7

One way to characterize the state of being towards which we are striving is to say that it is a state of enkindlement. As we focus our thoughts and energy on teaching, then, we should remember that the fire of love for Bahá'u'lláh in our hearts should burn brighter and brighter each day.

Commit to memory the following passage from the Writings of 'Abdu'l-Bahá, and let it remind you always of the need to feed the flame of the love of God in your heart so that its warmth can be felt by all those who come into contact with you and its light may illumine their minds:

> **"O thou lamp who art enkindled with the fire of the Love of God! Verily, I read thy recent letter which showed thy strong love, thy being ablaze with the fire of the love of thy Lord, the Mighty, the Praised, and the penetration of the Spirit of Truth in thy limbs, nerves, veins, arteries, bones, blood and**

flesh, until it hath taken the reins of power from thy hands and moveth thee as it willeth, causeth thee to speak in what it willeth and attracteth thee as it willeth. This is becoming of whatever heart is replenished with the spirit of the love of God. Thou shalt surely behold wondrous traces and shalt discover the signs of thy Mighty Lord." [6]

SECTION 8

The passage you have just studied describes a state in which the believer cannot but help to serve and to teach the Cause. So infused is the Spirit of Truth into his very being that it takes the reins of power from him and moves him as it wills. Try to think, now, of the consequences of resisting such a natural impulse to teach.

1. What happens to a fountain that receives water but refuses to flow?

2. What happens to a person who constantly receives the bounties of God yet refuses to share them with others?

3. What happens to one who receives knowledge and refuses to teach?

SECTION 9

As you contemplate becoming more and more enkindled with the love of God, you should bear in mind that "being" and "doing" are two complementary aspects of Bahá'í life. So tightly interwoven are they that it is futile to attempt to separate them. We cannot wait all our lives until we live in a state of total enkindlement before we teach. Even the smallest of flames gives warmth and light. There are many things that we should do simultaneously. We must pray and meditate on the profound meaning of the Writings we study each day. We must strive to purify our hearts and reflect His attributes. We must open our inner eyes, behold His beauty and become enamored with it. And we must be active in the field of service and teach His Cause. Aware of the interconnectedness between "being" and "doing", which of the following statements would you make without hesitation? Mark them.

____ All I have to do is concentrate on loving Bahá'u'lláh. Then I won't have to say a word. So enkindled will be my heart that people will wonder why I am the way I am. When they find out it is because I'm a Bahá'í, they will investigate and accept the Faith by themselves.

____ Although I am inadequate, I will carry out my duty to teach the Cause. Sharing the Message of Bahá'u'lláh with others helps increase my love for Him.

____ If I say the right things to a seeker, it doesn't make any difference whether my soul is enkindled or not.

____ Teaching is a state of being. It will come naturally. Why make an effort to teach!

____ I have found that, like all things in life, fulfilling my duty to teach the Cause takes discipline. Not only do I need discipline to improve my inner condition, but also to carry through with my good intentions and set aside time for teaching activities.

____ Teaching is a natural state of being. There is no need to make systematic plans. You should just let it happen!

SECTION 10

We have agreed that we can and should teach the Faith from the very moment we recognize Bahá'u'lláh. The image we have used is of a flame which, no matter how small, still gives light and warmth. At the same time we understand that without allowing our teaching efforts to ever slacken, we must constantly strive to enrich our spiritual life, feeding the fire of the love of God in our hearts and increasing its intensity. Let us pause and reflect, then, on that which increases enkindlement.

Below are two sets of statements. The first set includes statements which, while containing some truth, cause confusion on this matter. Match each to the statement in the second set that you find more suitable.

____ Knowledge is a veil. Too much knowledge leads to pride. Don't emphasize the study of the Writings. It is sufficient to concentrate on loving God and humanity.

____ So essential is enkindlement that one should withdraw from all activity for some time and work solely on one's inner condition.

a. The act of teaching, in itself, increases one's enkindlement.

b. Ultimately, one's enkindlement increases through the grace of God. However, this does not imply that effort is not needed. Praying daily, supplicating at His Threshold, reading the Writings, and actively serving Him—these open the doors of the soul to receive God's grace and bounties.

____ When one is enkindled with the fire of the love of God, one lives in a state of joy and feels no pain.

____ We fail to obey the laws of God because we don't love Bahá'u'lláh enough.

____ Enkindlement only comes through the grace of God. Therefore, we need not make any effort to increase its intensity.

____ Once the flame of the love of God has been lit in one's heart, it can never be put out. It will work within the heart by itself and purify it.

c. Knowledge feeds the flame of love for Bahá'u'lláh in one's heart. The more one comes to know Him through the study of His Revelation, the more deeply one loves Him. If one is freed from ego, which can lead to pride and turn knowledge into a veil, the acquisition of knowledge can be an important factor in increasing one's enkindlement.

d. Just as prayer and service to the Cause help to increase the flame of the love of God in one's heart, the winds of ego and selfish desires quench it. Therefore, one must be vigilant and protect the flame of the love of God in one's heart.

e. Sacrifice is essential for spiritual growth, and it entails pain. But God brings joy. One should joyfully accept the pain that one feels as the veils of self are burned away by the fire of the love of God.

f. Even when we love Bahá'u'lláh we can make many mistakes, for we are weak and are in constant need of His Mercy and Forgiveness. Making an effort to obey His laws increases enkindlement.

Now write a short paragraph describing in your own words how enkindlement is increased.

_____
_____
_____
_____
_____
_____
_____
_____
_____
_____

SECTION 11

Having explored the concept of duty in some detail, let us study a few passages in which Bahá'u'lláh clearly enjoins upon us the duty of teaching His Cause. Memorize as many of the passages as you can:

> "Say: To assist Me is to teach My Cause. This is a theme with which whole Tablets are laden. This is the changeless commandment of God, eternal in the past, eternal in the future." [7]

> "Be not dismayed, O peoples of the world, when the daystar of My beauty is set, and the heaven of My tabernacle is concealed from your eyes. Arise to further My Cause, and to exalt My Word amongst men. We are with you at all times, and shall strengthen you through the power of truth." [8]

> "The Pen of the Most High hath decreed and imposed upon every one the obligation to teach this Cause. . . . God will, no doubt, inspire whosoever detacheth himself from all else but Him, and will cause the pure waters of wisdom and utterance to gush out and flow copiously from his heart." [9]

> "God hath prescribed unto every one the duty of teaching His Cause. Whoever ariseth to discharge this duty, must needs, ere he proclaimeth His Message, adorn himself with the ornament of an upright and praiseworthy character, so that his words may attract the hearts of such as are receptive to his call." [10]

> "O ye beloved of God! Repose not yourselves on your couches, nay bestir yourselves as soon as ye recognize your Lord, the Creator, and hear of the things which have befallen Him, and hasten to His assistance. Unloose your tongues, and proclaim unceasingly His Cause. This shall be better for you than all the treasures of the past and of the future, if ye be of them that comprehend this truth." [11]

The Spiritual Nature of Teaching - 15

SECTION 12

When considering the various aspects of our duty to teach, we must not forget that the commandments of God are a sign of His bounty to us. Not for a moment should we think that we are doing God a favor by obeying His commandments. He could, with a single word, secure the complete victory of His Cause. That He has given us the opportunity to spread His Faith is an inestimable blessing which has been conferred upon each one of us. Bahá'u'lláh says:

> "If it be Our pleasure We shall render the Cause victorious through the power of a single word from Our presence. He is in truth the Omnipotent, the All-Compelling. Should it be God's intention, there would appear out of the forests of celestial might the lion of indomitable strength whose roaring is like unto the peals of thunder reverberating in the mountains. However, since Our loving providence surpasseth all things, We have ordained that complete victory should be achieved through speech and utterance, that Our servants throughout the earth may thereby become the recipients of divine good. This is but a token of God's bounty vouchsafed unto them." 12

In spoken and written language, metaphors are often employed to convey an idea, that is, a word or phrase which brings to mind a certain image is used to describe something else. In this passage, Bahá'u'lláh uses the metaphor of a lion. The lion emerges from the forests of celestial might, and his roar is like thunder echoing in the mountains. This image gives us a glimpse of the power of God, the Creator. Through a single act, He could make His Might known and all the peoples of the earth would bow down in submission before Him. It is only out of His loving-kindness that He allows us, His servants, to be the instruments for the diffusion of His Faith. Complete the following sentences using words and phrases from the quotation:

1. If it be God's pleasure, He could _____ .

2. If it be God's intention, there would *appear out of the forest of celestial might...* .

3. The roaring of this lion would be like *peals of thunder* .

4. However, since His loving providence surpasses all things, God has ordained that *complete victory* .

5. This He has done so that *the earth may thereby become the recipients of Divine good.*

6. This is but *a token of god's bounty* .

16 - The Spiritual Nature of Teaching

SECTION 13

Now that you have thought about the significance of teaching as a duty prescribed unto us by God, it is suggested you carry out the exercise below.

It is not uncommon for people to hold certain beliefs and, at the same time, say things that basically contradict those beliefs. In general, it is not easy to be consistent. We all have habits of the mind, formed throughout our lives, that cause us to say things without thinking about them. If we did, it would become clear to us that we do not really believe some of the statements we make. As we acquire knowledge, then, it is worthwhile to pause from time to time and examine the validity of a few commonly made statements in the light of our new understanding. Decide which of the following statements are consistent with your understanding of the concept of teaching as a duty. Mark them.

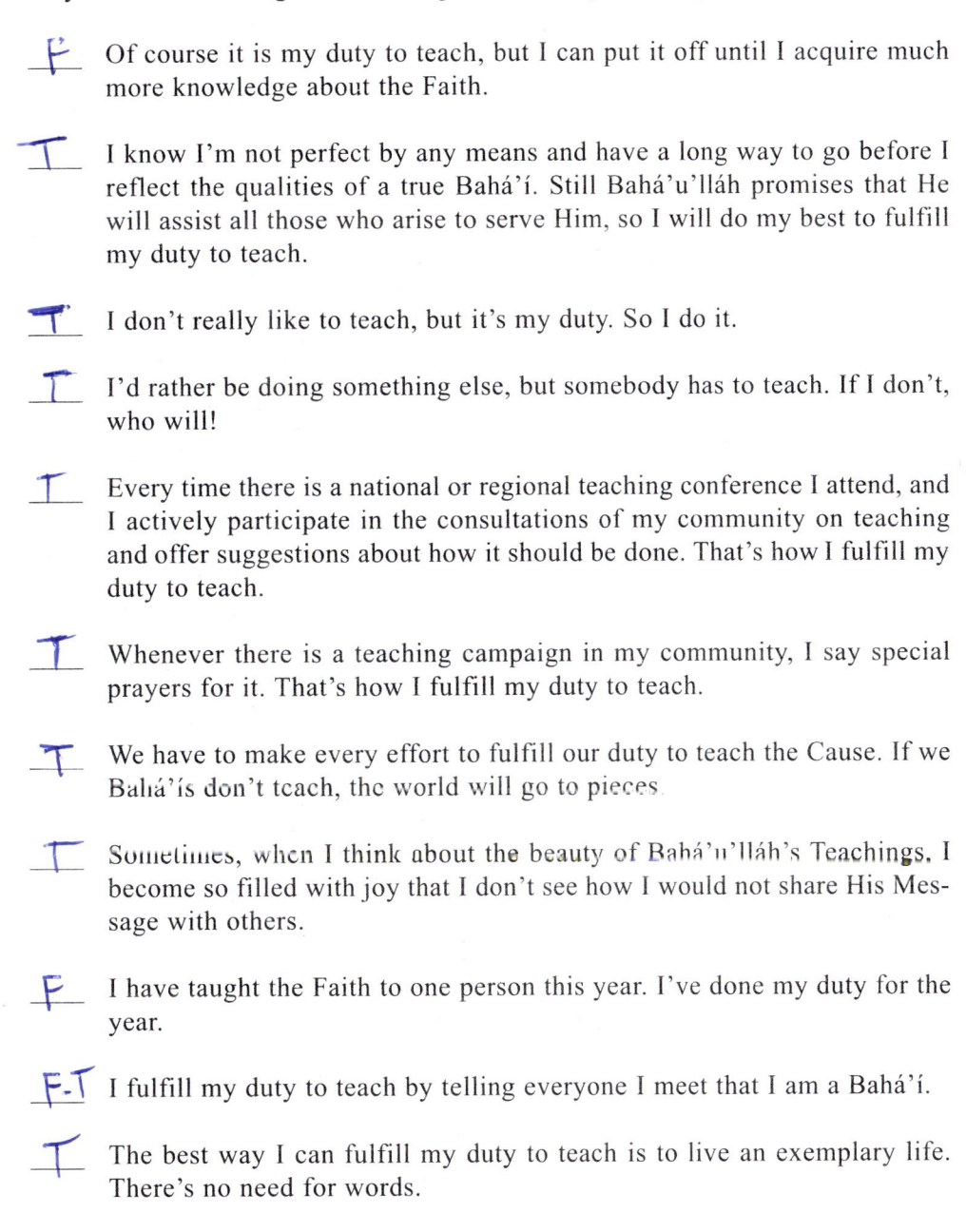

- **F** Of course it is my duty to teach, but I can put it off until I acquire much more knowledge about the Faith.

- **T** I know I'm not perfect by any means and have a long way to go before I reflect the qualities of a true Bahá'í. Still Bahá'u'lláh promises that He will assist all those who arise to serve Him, so I will do my best to fulfill my duty to teach.

- **T** I don't really like to teach, but it's my duty. So I do it.

- **T** I'd rather be doing something else, but somebody has to teach. If I don't, who will!

- **T** Every time there is a national or regional teaching conference I attend, and I actively participate in the consultations of my community on teaching and offer suggestions about how it should be done. That's how I fulfill my duty to teach.

- **T** Whenever there is a teaching campaign in my community, I say special prayers for it. That's how I fulfill my duty to teach.

- **T** We have to make every effort to fulfill our duty to teach the Cause. If we Bahá'ís don't teach, the world will go to pieces.

- **T** Sometimes, when I think about the beauty of Bahá'u'lláh's Teachings, I become so filled with joy that I don't see how I would not share His Message with others.

- **F** I have taught the Faith to one person this year. I've done my duty for the year.

- **F-T** I fulfill my duty to teach by telling everyone I meet that I am a Bahá'í.

- **T** The best way I can fulfill my duty to teach is to live an exemplary life. There's no need for words.

The Spiritual Nature of Teaching - 17

- __T__ I try to obey all the commandments of Bahá'u'lláh, including the one to teach His Cause, for only in this way will I be able to live an exemplary life.

- __F__ I know Bahá'u'lláh has enjoined the duty of teaching His Cause on every one of His followers. But He didn't really mean "everyone". Pioneers, traveling teachers, the members of the institutions—they're the real teachers of the Cause.

- __T__ I fulfill my duty to teach the Cause because, in that way, I will receive God's manifold bounties and favors.

- __T__ I fulfill my duty to teach the Cause because of my love for humanity.

- __T__ I fulfill my duty to teach the Cause because of my love for Bahá'u'lláh.

Memorize the following passage from a Tablet revealed by 'Abdu'l-Bahá:

> **"O thou seeker of the kingdom of God! If thou wishest thy speech and utterance to take effect in the hardened hearts, be thou severed from all attachment to this world and turn unto the Kingdom of God. Enkindle the fire of the love of God in the heart with such intensity that thou mayest become a flame of fire and a luminous lamp of guidance. At that time thy speech will take effect within the hearts, through the confirmation of the Holy Spirit."** [13]

SECTION 14

In the quotation we studied in Section 6, the Guardian tells us that teaching is a "sacred" duty. In what sense is it sacred? Of course, the mere fact that teaching is a commandment of God makes this duty sacred. But are there other dimensions of sacredness that we should explore in relation to teaching? In one of His Tablets Bahá'u'lláh says:

> **"That which He hath reserved for Himself are the cities of men's hearts; and of these the loved ones of Him Who is the Sovereign Truth are, in this Day, as the keys. Please God they may, one and all, be enabled to unlock, through the power of the Most Great Name, the gates of these cities."** [14]

In another passage He states:

> **"The things He hath reserved for Himself are the cities of men's hearts, that He may cleanse them from all earthly defilements, and enable them to draw nigh unto the hallowed Spot which the hands of the infidel can never profane. Open, O people, the city of the human heart with the key of your utterance. Thus have We, according to a pre-ordained measure, prescribed unto you your duty."** [15]

Imp

Answering the following questions will help you to see how these passages relate to sacredness and the act of teaching:

1. What has God reserved for Himself? _The cities of m—_

2. What word do we use to describe "that which belongs to God"? _____

3. Who are the keys to the cities of men's hearts? _____

4. What does God wish to do with these cities? _____

5. What place has He destined for these hearts? _Hallowed spot_

6. With what key are we to open the city of the human heart? _____

7. What duty has been prescribed unto us in these passages? _____

8. Now complete the following sentence:
Teaching is _a commandment of God_ _____.

SECTION 15

There is yet another dimension to sacredness we need to consider in our effort to explore its relation to teaching. In one of His Tablets Bahá'u'lláh refers to His Revelation in these words:

> "Say: This is the sealed and mystic Scroll, the repository of God's irrevocable Decree, bearing the words which the Finger of Holiness hath traced, that lay wrapt within the veil of impenetrable mystery, and hath now been sent down as a token of the grace of Him Who is the Almighty, the Ancient of Days. In it have We decreed the destinies of all the dwellers of the earth and the denizens of heaven, and written down the knowledge of all things from first to last." [16]

In this passage, Bahá'u'lláh describes His Revelation as a sealed and mystic Scroll. A scroll is a roll of paper on which an important message is written. This sealed and mystic Scroll is the repository of God's Decree, that is, it carries that which God has commanded and is unchangeable. The following exercise should help you gain insights into the meaning of this passage. Fill in the blanks using words from the quotation and then read the sentences together.

1. Bahá'u'lláh's Revelation has been sent down to us as a token of God's __grace__.

2. That which has been sent down is the __Sealed__ and __mystic__ Scroll that before lay wrapt within the _____ of _____.

3. It is the repository of God's __irrevocable Decree__.

4. In it God has decreed the destinies of all the __dwellers__ of the earth and heaven.

5. Bahá'u'lláh's Revelation contains in it the __knowledge__ of all things from __first__ to __last__.

SECTION 16

Consider now what we have studied in the previous two sections. Teaching is the sacred duty of every Bahá'í, for it is enjoined upon us by God. Moreover, when we teach we are dealing with two very sacred things. One is the human heart which essentially belongs to God. Teaching, in fact, can be described as that spiritual act which results in the opening of the city of the human heart to Him. The other sacred thing with which teaching is concerned is the Revelation of Bahá'u'lláh. We teach in order to connect the heart to His Revelation, His greatest bestowal to humankind.

Try to remember occasions in your life when you felt the presence of the sacred. If you have ever been in the Holy Shrines of Bahá'u'lláh and the Báb, you retain strong memories of how it felt to draw close to, and bow down at, their Sacred Thresholds. But even if you have not yet had that bounty, there must be many occasions in your life when you were enraptured in prayer, with your mind and heart turned towards God, and you vividly felt to be standing in His presence. What are some of the sentiments that fill your heart in such moments? Check them in the following list:

✓ Intense love	✗ Pride	✓ Joy
✓ Awe	✗ Uneasiness	✗ Unworthiness
✗ Indifference	✓ Freedom	✓ Reverence
✓ Submissiveness	✓ Gratitude	✓ Peace

SECTION 17

This last exercise has reminded us of the respectful attitude that one assumes when approaching that which is sacred and of the noble feelings that stir in one's heart when standing in the presence of the sacred. In this context, an important question must be asked: How does your own awareness of the sacred nature of teaching increase your effectiveness as a teacher of the Cause? To help you answer this question, it is suggested that you carry out the exercise below in which three different ways to view the act of teaching are described, and you are asked to think about the results of each. Do not worry that the situation presented is somewhat artificial. The exercise will, nonetheless, provide you with certain needed insights.

> Suppose that in a relatively short period of time you succeeded in helping thirty people embrace the Cause of Bahá'u'lláh and enroll in the community. These thirty people were all from the same background and extremely receptive to the Faith. Therefore, your presentation of the Message to them was basically the same. It consisted in explaining to them, in appropriate detail, the fundamental verities enshrined in the Revelation of Bahá'u'lláh and in helping them to recognize Him as the Manifestation of God for today. You also made sure they understood the implications of entering into the shelter of the Covenant. Moreover, in every instance, you carried out your duty to teach with the utmost sincerity, and solely for the sake of love for Bahá'u'lláh.
>
> Yet your own perception of what you were doing was not constant in all cases. At first you saw yourself more or less as a salesman. "Teaching is like selling," you would tell yourself. "The Faith has the best ideas around. I am a good teacher if I can effectively package the Faith and sell these wonderful ideas to people."
>
> By the time ten people had enrolled in the Faith, your view of teaching had changed. You had attended a lecture about the horrible state of the world and had become aware that the Faith was the answer to humanity's ills. What was needed, you felt, was to recruit as many people as quickly as possible—people who would work for the establishment of unity, for the elimination of prejudices, and for the cause of justice. So that was how you viewed your own efforts to teach, and you enthusiastically began to invite others to join a movement with great and important ideals—peace, unity, the equality of the sexes, the abolition of prejudices, and the eradication of poverty and suffering.
>
> After having taught ten new people the Faith in this way, you became familiar with some of the quotations we have studied in this unit. While you were still concerned with the condition of the world and felt that it was important to increase the number of people who could apply Bahá'u'lláh's Teachings to transform it, the foremost thought in your mind each time you explained the Faith to someone was that you were addressing a human heart which belongs to God and therefore is sacred. What you were doing, you would say to yourself, was using the key of utterance to open the gates to the city of this heart. Under these conditions the last ten people declared their faith in Bahá'u'lláh.
>
> Having helped to enroll these thirty friends, you now embark on a systematic program to deepen them in order to assist them in becoming active supporters of the Faith. Do you think there will be any difference in the degree to which the three groups respond to the deepening program? Will your deepening efforts be more effective with any one group? Of course, there will be differences among the individual friends, for, from any one of the three groups could emerge an individual so prepared by Bahá'u'lláh, so eager to delve into His Revelation, that he or she rapidly becomes deepened and involved in the affairs of the community. What you

are being asked is to think about each group as a whole. On average, do you think there will be any significant difference between the three? Discuss this question in your group and write your conclusions down below.

SECTION 18

When the gates to the city of the human heart are opened and the heart is connected to Bahá'u'lláh's Revelation, a profound process of transformation begins. This transformation does not take place instantly, but occurs continually throughout our lives. Still, the importance that the act of accepting Bahá'u'lláh has for this process of transformation should never be underestimated. Recognizing the Sun of Truth and allowing its rays to enter and illumine the heart is the single most significant step that a person can take in his or her life. By reflecting on the transformation that follows recognition of Bahá'u'lláh, we are better able to understand how we can help others take this important first step. Can you write one or two sentences about some of the changes that occur in each of the following once we accept Bahá'u'lláh and begin to apply His Teachings:

1. Our hearts: _____
   _____
   _____

2. Our minds: _____
   _____
   _____

3. Our thoughts: _____
   _____
   _____

4. Our character: _____
   _____
   _____

5. Our relations with other human beings: _____
   _____
   _____

6. Our goals in life: _____
   _____
   _____

7. Our view of the world: _____
   _____
   _____

As a teacher of the Cause, you have an important role to play in helping a person to take the first step of recognizing Bahá'u'lláh. You will also support him or her at least through those initial stages of transformation. But how can you fulfill such an extraordinary task?

SECTION 19

In the physical world, change occurs through the application of power. For us to move from one point to another, for a plant to grow, for a lamp to turn darkness into light, for the rivers to flow, and for the tides to rise and ebb, power is needed—the power supplied by the muscles of the human body, the power generated by the sun, by electricity, or by the gravitational force. It is important to ask, then, what are the powers that bring about the kind of transformation you have described in the previous section? So crucial is this question to our understanding of the spiritual nature of teaching that we will dedicate the rest of this unit to seeking answers to it. To begin, decide which of the following powers can contribute to spiritual transformation:

- ____ The power of prayer
- ____ The power of pure and goodly deeds
- ____ The power of the Word of God
- ____ The power of justice
- ____ The power of the sword
- ____ The power of unity
- ____ The power of truth
- ____ The power of example
- ____ The power of kindly words
- ____ The power of convincing arguments
- ____ The power of money
- ____ The power of a righteous character
- ____ The power of the Covenant
- ____ The power of political domination
- ____ The power of protest
- ____ The power of love
- ____ The power of persuasion
- ____ The power of faith
- ____ The power of positive thoughts
- ____ The power of the gun
- ____ The power of true knowledge
- ____ The power of reason
- ____ The power of science
- ____ The power of intimidation

SECTION 20

From among all the powers that contribute to spiritual transformation one stands out as unique, as the fundamental force behind the other powers. Which is it?

Throughout the centuries, there has been a belief in the existence of a substance called an "elixir" which once applied to copper, or in fact to any other element, would turn it into gold. This process, which has been sought by many but never found, is referred to as the transmutation of elements. In one of His Tablets, Bahá'u'lláh uses this image to reveal a most profound spiritual truth:

"The vitality of men's belief in God is dying out in every land; nothing short of His wholesome medicine can ever restore it. The corrosion of ungodliness is eating into the vitals of human society; what else but the Elixir of His potent Revelation can cleanse and revive it? Is it within human power, O Hakím, to effect in the constituent elements of any of the minute and indivisible particles of matter so complete a transformation as to transmute it into purest gold? Perplexing and difficult as this may appear, the still greater task of converting satanic strength into heavenly power is one that We have been empowered to accomplish. The

Force capable of such a transformation transcendeth the potency of the Elixir itself. The Word of God, alone, can claim the distinction of being endowed with the capacity required for so great and far-reaching a change."[17]

Now that you have read this passage, which power would you say stands out as unique, as the fundamental force behind all other powers? _____

SECTION 21

In the above passage, we are told that, difficult as the transmutation of an element into pure gold may be, changing satanic strength into heavenly power is surely more formidable. Yet the Word of God, and the Word of God alone, can bring about such a fundamental transformation. But what is the "Word of God", we must ask, which is capable of so stupendous an accomplishment? Bahá'u'lláh says:

> "Know thou, moreover, that the Word of God—exalted be His glory—is higher and far superior to that which the senses can perceive, for it is sanctified from any property or substance. It transcendeth the limitations of known elements and is exalted above all the essential and recognized substances. It became manifest without any syllable or sound and is none but the Command of God which pervadeth all created things. It hath never been withheld from the world of being. It is God's all-pervasive grace, from which all grace doth emanate. It is an entity far removed above all that hath been and shall be."[18]

1. The Word of God is _higher_ and far _superior_ to that which the senses can perceive.

2. The Word of God is _sanctified_ from any _property_ or _substance_.

3. The Word of God _transcendeth_ the limitations of _known elements_.

4. The Word of God is _exalted_ above all the _essential_ and _recognized_ substances.

5. The Word of God became manifest without any _syllable_ or _sound_.

6. The Word of God is the _Command_ of God.

7. The Word of God, His Command, pervades _all created things_.

8. The Word of God, His Command, has never been _withheld_ from the _the world of being_.

9. The Word of God is His all-pervasive __grace__, from which __all grace__ emanates.

10. The Word of God is an entity __far removed__ above all that __hath been__ and all that __shall be__.

SECTION 22

Another image that gives us a glimpse of the power of the Word of God is that of the joining of the letters B and E. In the Writings we are told that God joined the letters B and E together, and issued the command "BE". Thus the whole of creation came into being. In a prayer Bahá'u'lláh has revealed:

> "How can, then, such a man succeed in befittingly extolling the One through a motion of Whose finger all the names and their kingdom were called into being, and all the attributes and their dominion were created, and Who, through yet another motion of that same finger, hath united the letters B and E (Be) and knit them together, manifesting thereby what the highest thoughts of Thy chosen ones who enjoy near access to Thee are unable to grasp, and what the profoundest wisdom of those of Thy loved ones that are wholly devoted to Thee are powerless to fathom." [19]

You may wish to memorize this passage.

SECTION 23

We have now learned that the Word of God is His all-pervasive Command and Grace, and is not made of syllables and sounds. Yet there do exist words that we can read and hear which carry with them the power of the Word of God, namely, those uttered by the Manifestation. These have the power to create, to regenerate and to transform, and for this reason, they are referred to as the "Creative Word". Bahá'u'lláh tells us:

> "Every word that proceedeth out of the mouth of God is endowed with such potency as can instill new life into every human frame, if ye be of them that comprehend this truth." [20]

> "O friend of mine! The Word of God is the king of words and its pervasive influence is incalculable. It hath ever dominated and will continue to dominate the realm of being. The Great Being saith: The Word is the master key for the whole world, inasmuch as through its potency the doors of the hearts of men, which in reality are the doors of heaven, are unlocked." [21]

Below are several questions which refer to the quotations in this section, as well as in the preceding ones. Although some of the questions only require you to respond "yes" or "no", completing the entire exercise should help clarify your understanding of the power of the Word of God.

1. Is the Word of God made of syllables and sounds? _____

2. Is the Word of God made of any known substance? _____

3. Can the Word of God be perceived by our senses? _____

4. What is the Word of God?
   a. _____
   b. _____

5. What does it mean that the Command of God pervades all created things? _____
   _____
   _____

6. Would anything in the universe exist if it were not called into being by the Command of God? _____

7. What does it mean that the grace of God is all-pervasive? _____
   _____

8. What would happen if God's grace were withheld from the world of being? ___
   _____
   _____

9. Since the Word of God cannot be perceived by our senses and faculties, how do we become aware of it? _____

10. Who is "the mouth of God" through whom God speaks? _____

11. With what is every word uttered by the Manifestation of God endowed? _____
    _____

12. What are some of the characteristics of the "new life" instilled into every human being by the Word of God? _____
    _____
    _____
    _____

13. How great is the influence of the Word of God? _____

14. What is the master key to the whole world? _____

15. What does the Word of God do to the hearts of people? _____

Now memorize the following quotation:

> "This is the day in which to speak. It is incumbent upon the people of Bahá to strive, with the utmost patience and forbearance, to guide the peoples of the world to the Most Great Horizon. Every body calleth aloud for a soul. Heavenly souls must needs quicken, with the breath of the Word of God, the dead bodies with a fresh spirit." [22]

SECTION 24

Let us examine the relationship between some of the ideas we have discussed in the previous sections. Bahá'u'lláh commands us to open the city of the human heart with the key of our utterance. Once the gates to this city are opened, a wondrous transformation begins to occur. Among the powers that drive this transformation, the power of the Word of God, conveyed through the words of the Manifestation, is most indispensable. Does this mean, then, that it is best for us not to use our own words in teaching and merely recite to others passages from the Writings of Bahá'u'lláh?

In answering this question remind yourself of the behavior of certain religious zealots who carry around with them a copy of a Holy Book, from which they constantly preach at people. Certainly we would not expect such behavior from a Bahá'í teacher. Yet we must learn to draw upon the power of the Word of God in our teaching efforts. Bahá'u'lláh thus exhorts us:

> "The sanctified souls should ponder and meditate in their hearts regarding the methods of teaching. From the texts of the wondrous, heavenly Scriptures they should memorize phrases and passages bearing on various instances, so that in the course of their speech they may recite divine verses whenever the occasion demandeth it, inasmuch as these holy verses are the most potent elixir, the greatest and mightiest talisman. So potent is their influence that the hearer will have no cause for vacillation." [23]

1. Bahá'u'lláh tells us to __ponder__ and __meditate__ in our hearts regarding the __methods__ of __teaching__.

2. We should __memorize__ phrases and __passages__ related to various subjects from the __texts__ of the Holy Scriptures.

3. We should memorize passages from the Holy Scriptures so that in the _course_ of our _speech_ we may _recite_ divine verses whenever _the occasion demandeth it_.

4. We should recite divine verses in our speech inasmuch as these _these holy verses_ are the most potent _elixir_.

5. So _potent_ is the _influence_ of the holy verses that the _hearer_ will have no cause for _vacillation_.

SECTION 25

Bahá'u'lláh tells us to memorize phrases and passages from the Holy Scriptures in order that we may use them in our speech whenever the opportunity arises. Clearly this refers first and foremost to His own Writings, for He is the Manifestation of God for today and, like those of all the previous Manifestations such as the Báb, His utterances constitute the Creative Word.

But what about the words of 'Abdu'l-Bahá? In your group, discuss the power that His words exert on the listener. Although His Writings may not be considered divinely revealed verses, are they the same as those of any other human being, or do they possess a station of their own? From where do His words draw their power? Is it not desirable for us to quote passages from His Writings in our speech, as we do from the Writings of Bahá'u'lláh?

Now consider the same set of questions in relation to the writings of the Guardian. After having done so, carry out a similar discussion regarding the guidance of the Universal House of Justice.

SECTION 26

We have seen the importance of memorizing passages from the writings and incorporating them into our speech. Yet we also know that in explaining Bahá'u'lláh's Teachings, we need to use our own words as well, for we cannot simply quote passage after passage from the Scriptures to people. Quotations should be woven into our conversations and discussions in a natural way. The question is, then: How can we make sure that we touch the hearts of our listeners and help them to understand the Message of Bahá'u'lláh and reach the shores of the Ocean of His Revelation?

Clearly the answer is that, although we use our own words, what we say should be entirely in keeping with the Teachings. It is not our own theories that we should be giving, but Bahá'u'lláh's Message in the purest form possible. This, of course, requires us to immerse ourselves in the writings and to constantly deepen our knowledge and understanding of the Faith. Regarding the importance of deepening, the Guardian has said:

"Surely the ideal way of teaching is to prove our points by constant reference to the actual words of Bahá'u'lláh and the Master. This will save the Cause from being misinterpreted by individuals. It is what these divine Lights say that is truth and therefore They should be the authorities of our statements.

"This, however, does not mean that our freedom of expression is limited. We can always find new ways of approach to that truth or explain how they influence our life and condition. The more deep our studies the more we can understand the significance of the Teachings." [24]

"To deepen in the Cause means to read the Writings of Bahá'u'lláh and the Master so thoroughly as to be able to give it to others in its pure form. There are many who have some superficial idea of what the Cause stands for. They, therefore, present it together with all sorts of ideas that are their own. As the Cause is still in its early days we must be most careful lest we fall under this error and injure the Movement we so much adore.

"There is no limit to the study of the Cause. The more we read the writings the more truths we can find in them and the more we will see that our previous notions were erroneous." [25]

Now read the following statements and decide if they are true or false. Do not be content with simply marking the answers. The sequence of ideas should help you think about the importance of studying the writings systematically.

1. The study of the writings is only for the highly educated. Others merely need to have the essence of things explained to them in simple terms. T ☐ F ☐

2. Every Bahá'í should study the writings. Even people not accustomed to reading can study, with the help of others, one passage at a time. T ☐ F ☐

3. As we study the writings and gain deeper and deeper understanding of the Faith, we are able to express faithfully the truths enshrined in the Revelation, and therefore our words will have greater effect on the listener. T ☐ F ☐

4. Even if we study the writings so well that we learn to present the Faith in a pure form, our own words can can never be a substitute for the Creative Word, which has a special power and penetrates the hearts of men. T ☐ F ☐

5. By trying to be faithful to the writings when teaching the Cause, we put limits on our own freedom of thinking and expression. T ☐ F ☐

6. If we are faithful to the writings when teaching the Cause, our thoughts are raised to a higher level; we are no longer slaves to the opinions of men and restricted by narrow thoughts. T ☐ F ☐

7. If we are faithful to the writings when teaching the Cause, we will be inspired, and insights and answers come to our mind that we never could have thought of before. T ☐ F ☐

8. Once you have read a book or tablet revealed by one of the Central Figures of the Faith, there's no point in rereading it. T ☐ F ☐

9. No matter how many times one reads any passage from the writings, one finds new meaning and fresh insights in it. T ☐ F ☐

10. One does not study the writings simply to accumulate volumes of information about the Faith. What matters is how much one reflects on the writings and strives to understand the meaning enshrined therein. T ☐ F ☐

11. Deepening is a personal matter and something one does alone. T ☐ F ☐

12. Deepening is a personal matter and something one only does alone. T ☐ F ☐

13. The study of the writings should not merely be carried out as a personal habit; it must also be the systematic pursuit of groups and communities. T ☐ F ☐

14. When we teach the Faith, it is important to avoid mixing into our presentation all sorts of ideas of our own. Therefore, we should not teach until we know all the writings. T ☐ F ☐

15. We cannot wait until we are fully deepened before we teach. Deepening our knowledge of the Faith is to be carried out parallel to our teaching efforts. Otherwise we would never teach, because we can never be deepened enough. T ☐ F ☐

SECTION 27

Bringing our words into conformity with the Teachings of Bahá'u'lláh as interpreted by 'Abdu'l-Bahá and the Guardian, and with the guidance we receive from the Universal House of Justice, endows them with great power. This power is multiplied if we actually learn passages from the writings and weave them into our speech naturally and with wisdom. But our words must satisfy other conditions if they are to touch the hearts of those we teach. Particularly, they must carry with them the force of love, love that is genuinely felt, not a mere appearance of love. In one of His talks, 'Abdu'l-Bahá stated:

> **"If I love you, I need not continually speak of my love—you will know without any words. On the other hand if I love you not, that also will you know—and you would not believe me, were I to tell you in a thousand words, that I loved you."** [26]

Love is not simply some abstract principle that one talks about. It is real, and it is directed towards something or someone. And when love is a reality, when one truly loves another, a bond is created between hearts through which noble feelings and lofty ideas can flow. One soul can uplift the other, and joy fills them both.

Mírzá Abu'l-Faḍl, a Bahá'í teacher in whom 'Abdu'l-Bahá placed the greatest trust, once analyzed the concept of love for humanity in a talk given to a group of friends. He explained how easy it is for any one of us to sit comfortably in a house with a nice garden and say "I love humanity." But, according to Mírzá Abu'l-Faḍl, love only becomes real when it is tested. Only when we have fought the battles of love and have time and again been wounded for the sake of love, can we utter the sentence "I love" with authority and assurance. So, he said, a person who wants to create love within himself must test himself and see if he meets all the conditions of true love.

What are some of these conditions? Clearly they include sincerity and truthfulness, generosity and liberality, forgiveness and trustworthiness. You can readily see that all of these are necessary for love to exist. For what is insincere love but hypocrisy? What is the outcome of love when it is ruled by jealousy and control, and not by open-heartedness and generosity? What kind of love is associated with vengeance rather than forgiveness? How can anyone trust in our love, if we are not trustworthy?

With this understanding of love, let us now turn our attention to the act of teaching. When you teach the Cause, you are communicating with "someone". You do not just teach in abstract. Think about the feelings you have towards someone you love—a dear friend, your mother and father, brothers and sisters, husband or wife, your children. These feelings are very real. It would, of course, be unreasonable to believe that we could love a stranger with the same intensity as we love those who are near to us. What is essential to understand, however, is that by teaching we are expressing our love for humanity, and our love for humanity should be translated into concrete love for individual members of the human race. It is not enough for us to simply have some abstract love for an abstract idealization of humanity.

An important question to ask in this respect is: For what reason would a teacher of the Cause not love a person, even a stranger, who is, after all, listening to him or her explain the Message of Bahá'u'lláh? In contemplating this question, think of 'Abdu'l-Bahá. How did He love humanity? Did He not shower love and kindness upon each and every human being with whom He came into contact?

To increase your understanding of the power of love in teaching the Cause, decide whether the following statements are true or false:

1. Words are words. They have the same effect whether you say them with love in your heart or not. T ☐ F ☒

2. When words are clothed with love, they have greater effect on the listener's heart. T ☒ F ☐

3. We can only love someone we know, like our mother or father, or a dear friend. T ☐ F ☒

4. It is possible to love a person we hardly know. T ☒ F ☒

5. To show love to every human being is impossible unless you are some kind of a saint. T ☐ F ☒

6. Loving humanity means loving every human being with the same intensity. T ☒ F ☐

7. That a person you do not know takes the time to listen to what you are saying, in itself, stimulates love in your heart for him or her. T ☒ F ☐

8. It is contradictory to say: "I love humanity, but do not care to teach anyone and offer them the great bounties that result from accepting Bahá'u'lláh as the Manifestation of God for today." T ☒ F ☐

9. If we do not teach the Cause, it is because we do not have enough love for humanity. T ☒ F ☐

10. It is incorrect to say that those who do not teach the Cause do not love humanity. There may be other factors, such as fear, lack of confidence, or shyness, that prevent a person who is full of love from teaching. T ☐ F ☒

11. We should only teach our loved ones and not those we do not know. T ☐ F ☒

12. We should love all those we teach. T ☒ F ☐

13. Love for humanity is not the main reason for teaching. It is our love for God that compels us to take up this sacred duty. T ☒ F ☐

14. If we feel that we do not love humanity enough, we should not teach. T ☐ F ☒

15. The act of teaching increases our love for our fellow human beings. Therefore we should not make insufficient love an excuse for not teaching. T ☒ F ☐

SECTION 28

There are many ways of expressing love, and we have said that when we teach, we are translating our love for humanity into love for one or more of its individual members. The power of love, 'Abdu'l-Bahá tells us, must have a mode of expression and an object towards which it is directed, like the power of electricity which is made manifest in electric light. Without such means, love would be unseen, unheard, unfelt—all together unexpressed, unmanifested.

Although the power of love finds expression when it is directed towards a specific object, we should remember that love itself is not limited. Love is unlimited, boundless, infinite. 'Abdu'l-Bahá tell us that: **"When you love a member of your family or a compatriot, let it be with a ray of the Infinite Love! Let it be in God, and for God! Wherever you find the attributes of God love that person, whether he be of your family or of another. Shed the light of a boundless love on every human being whom you meet..."** [27] Memorize the following passage from the Writings of 'Abdu'l-Bahá:

"O thou son of the Kingdom! All things are beneficial if joined with the love of God; and without His love all things are harmful, and act as a veil between man and the Lord of the Kingdom. When His love is there, every bitterness turneth sweet, and every bounty rendereth a wholesome pleasure. For example, a melody, sweet to the ear, bringeth the very spirit of life to a heart in love with God, yet staineth with lust a soul engrossed in sensual desires. And every branch of learning, conjoined with the love of God, is approved and worthy of praise; but bereft of His love, learning is barren—indeed, it bringeth on madness. Every kind of knowledge, every science, is as a tree: if the fruit of it be the love of God, then is it a blessed tree, but if not, that tree is but dried-up wood, and shall only feed the fire." [28]

SECTION 29

To end this unit, we should remind ourselves of an important fact that we all have learned in our lives: that, without divine assistance, nothing can be achieved. When teaching the Cause, then, we have to be ever conscious of divine assistance and seek strength from the hosts of the Supreme Concourse. Below are only a few of the many passages from the Writings on this subject. You may wish to memorize them, if you have not already done so on earlier occasions.

"By the righteousness of God! Whoso openeth his lips in this Day and maketh mention of the name of his Lord, the hosts of Divine inspiration shall descend upon him from the heaven of My name, the All-Knowing, the All-Wise. On him shall also descend the Concourse on high, each bearing aloft a chalice of pure light. Thus hath it been foreordained in the realm of God's Revelation, by the behest of Him Who is the All-Glorious, the Most Powerful." [29]

"They that have forsaken their country for the purpose of teaching Our Cause—these shall the Faithful Spirit strengthen through its power. A company of Our chosen angels shall go forth with them, as bidden by Him Who is

the Almighty, the All-Wise. How great the blessedness that awaiteth him that hath attained the honor of serving the Almighty!" [30]

"He, verily, will aid everyone that aideth Him, and will remember everyone that remembereth Him. To this beareth witness this Tablet that hath shed the splendor of the loving-kindness of your Lord, the All-Glorious, the All-Compelling." [31]

"Say: Beware, O people of Bahá, lest the strong ones of the earth rob you of your strength, or they who rule the world fill you with fear. Put your trust in God, and commit your affairs to His keeping. He, verily, will, through the power of truth, render you victorious, and He, verily, is powerful to do what He willeth, and in His grasp are the reins of omnipotent might." [32]

"By God besides Whom is none other God! Should any one arise for the triumph of our Cause, him will God render victorious though tens of thousands of enemies be leagued against him. And if his love for Me wax stronger, God will establish his ascendancy over all the powers of earth and heaven. Thus have We breathed the spirit of power into all regions." [33]

"He will come to your aid with invisible hosts, and support you with armies of inspiration from the Concourse above; He will send unto you sweet perfumes from the highest Paradise, and waft over you the pure breathings that blow from the rose gardens of the Company on high. He will breathe into your hearts the spirit of life, cause you to enter the Ark of salvation, and reveal unto you His clear tokens and signs. Verily is this abounding grace. Verily is this the victory that none can deny." [34]

"O ye servants of the Sacred Threshold! The triumphant hosts of the Celestial Concourse, arrayed and marshaled in the Realms above, stand ready and expectant to assist and assure victory to that valiant horseman who with confidence spurs on his charger into the arena of service. Well is it with that fearless warrior, who armed with the power of true Knowledge, hastens unto the field, disperses the armies of ignorance, and scatters the hosts of error, who holds aloft the Standard of Divine Guidance, and sounds the Clarion of Victory. By the righteousness of the Lord! He hath achieved a glorious triumph and obtained the true victory." [35]

REFERENCES

1. *Gleanings from the Writings of Bahá'u'lláh* (Wilmette: Bahá'í Publishing Trust, 1983), CXXVIII, p. 278.

2. *Tablets of Abdul-Baha Abbas* (Chicago: Bahá'í Publishing Committee, 1930), vol. 1, p. 114.

3. *Tablets of Abdul-Baha Abbas* (Chicago: Bahá'í Publishing Committee, 1930), vol. 2, p. 473.

4. *Selections from the Writings of 'Abdu'l-Bahá* (Wilmette: Bahá'í Publishing Trust, 1997), no. 142, pp. 175-76.

5. From a letter dated 27 March 1933 written on behalf of Shoghi Effendi to a Local Spiritual Assembly, published in *Bahá'í News*, no. 73 (May 1933), p. 2.

6. *Tablets of Abdul-Baha Abbas* (Chicago: Bahá'í Publishing Committee, 1930), vol. 3, pp. 716-17.

7. *Tablets of Bahá'u'lláh Revealed after the Kitáb-i-Aqdas* (Wilmette: Bahá'í Publishing Trust, 1988), p. 196.

8. Bahá'u'lláh, *The Kitáb-i-Aqdas: The Most Holy Book* (Wilmette: Bahá'í Publishing Trust, 1993), p. 34.

9. *Gleanings from the Writings of Bahá'u'lláh*, CXLIV, p. 314.

10. Ibid., CLVIII, p. 335.

11. Ibid., CLIV, p. 330.

12. *Tablets of Bahá'u'lláh Revealed after the Kitáb-i-Aqdas*, pp. 197-98.

13. 'Abdu'l-Bahá, cited in *Star of the West*, vol. III, no. 19 (2 March 1913), p. 1.

14. *Gleanings from the Writings of Bahá'u'lláh*, CXV, pp. 241-42.

15. Ibid., CXXXIX, p. 304.

16. Ibid., CXXIX, pp. 281-82.

17. Ibid., XCIX, p. 200.

18. *Tablets of Bahá'u'lláh Revealed after the Kitáb-i-Aqdas*, pp. 140-41.

19. *Prayers and Meditations by Bahá'u'lláh* (Wilmette: Bahá'í Publishing Trust, 1987), p. 303.

20. *Gleanings from the Writings of Bahá'u'lláh,* LXXIV, p. 141.

21. *Tablets of Bahá'u'lláh Revealed after the Kitáb-i-Aqdas,* p. 173.

22. Bahá'u'lláh, cited in Shoghi Effendi, *The Advent of Divine Justice* (Wilmette: Bahá'í Publishing Trust, 1990), pp. 82-83.

23. *Tablets of Bahá'u'lláh Revealed after the Kitáb-i-Aqdas,* p. 200.

24. From a letter dated 16 February 1932 written on behalf of Shoghi Effendi to an individual believer, published in *The Importance of Deepening Our Knowledge and Understanding of the Faith,* comp. the Research Department of the Universal House of Justice (Wilmette: Bahá'í Publishing Trust, 1983), p. 32.

25. From a letter dated 25 April 1926 written on behalf of Shoghi Effendi to an individual believer, published in *The Importance of Deepening Our Knowledge and Understanding of the Faith,* pp. 28-29.

26. *Paris Talks: Addresses given by 'Abdu'l-Bahá in Paris in 1911-1912* (London: Bahá'í Publishing Trust, 1995), p. 3.

27. Ibid., p. 28.

28. *Selections from the Writings of 'Abdu'l-Bahá,* no. 154, p. 190.

29. *Gleanings from the Writings of Bahá'u'lláh,* CXXIX, p. 280.

30. Ibid., CLVII, p. 334.

31. Bahá'u'lláh, cited in *The Advent of Divine Justice,* p. 76.

32. Ibid., p. 82.

33. Bahá'u'lláh, cited in Shoghi Effendi, *The World Order of Bahá'u'lláh: Selected Letters* (Wilmette: Bahá'í Publishing Trust, 1991), p. 106.

34. *Selections from the Writings of 'Abdu'l-Bahá,* no. 157, p. 196.

35. Ibid., no. 208, pp. 276-77.

The Qualities and Attitudes of the Teacher

Purpose

To reflect on the qualities and attitudes of a teacher of the Cause.
To understand that effectiveness in teaching can be developed
if we approach it in a posture of learning—engaging in activity,
reflecting on what we have said and done,
and turning regularly to the writings
for insights and guidance.

SECTION 1

We fulfill the sacred duty enjoined upon us by Bahá'u'lláh to teach His Cause at least in two ways: by teaching those we seek out or with whom we come into contact in the course of our daily lives, and by participating in the teaching campaigns of our communities. In both contexts, we will have to be conscious of the fact, already emphasized in the first unit of this book, that "being" and "doing" are complementary and inseparable aspects of a spiritual life. Only if our efforts to teach others and to teach ourselves go hand in hand will we be able to reap a rich harvest. In a course on teaching, then, we need to dedicate the necessary time to explore the qualities and attitudes of a teacher.

What are some of the spiritual qualities that you must constantly strive to develop as you engage in regular and systematic teaching? In the sections that follow you will be presented with short quotations related to several spiritual qualities. The questions and exercises included in each section are to help you analyze how advancing in any one quality increases your effectiveness as a teacher of the Cause. The purpose of these sections, then, is not to undertake a general study of spiritual qualities but to examine them in the specific context of teaching. As a first step, list those qualities that you feel are most essential to success in teaching:

Patience - Empathy - Kindness - humility -

It is important to realize at this point that our discussions in the following sections will not be about attaining perfection itself, but about striving towards perfection. Without this realization, you will feel overwhelmed and discouraged, and will abandon any attempt to teach. For example, in the next section we will be concerned with how increasing purity of heart affects teaching, which is not to suggest that unless one is the essence of purity, one cannot be a teacher of the Cause. Naturally, the writings point us towards perfection, for if we are not aware of the goal how can we strive to achieve it?

SECTION 2

In the Tablets of the Divine Plan, 'Abdu'l-Bahá says:

> **"The aim is this: The intention of the teacher must be pure, his heart independent, his spirit attracted, his thought at peace, his resolution firm, his magnanimity exalted and in the love of God a shining torch."** [1]

In these same Tablets, He exhorts us:

> "... become ye sanctified above and purified from this world and the inhabitants thereof; suffer your intentions to work for the good of all; cut your attachment to the earth and like unto the essence of the spirit become ye light and delicate. Then with a firm resolution, a pure heart, a rejoiced spirit, and an eloquent tongue, engage your time in the promulgation of the divine principles..."[2]

Why do you think purity of heart and purity of intention contribute so much to success in teaching? What if our intentions are not pure but we are extremely good at pretending and convincing others that they are? Some of the impurities that come easily to mind in relation to teaching are a desire for recognition, ambition, and a sense of superiority towards those we teach. Can you explain how each of these affect teaching?

1. Sense of superiority: _____
   _____
   _____
   _____

2. Desire for recognition: _____
   _____
   _____
   _____

3. Ambition: _____
   _____
   _____
   _____

SECTION 3

In a letter written on his behalf, the Guardian has stated:

> "The Master assured us that when we forget ourselves, and strive with all our powers to serve and teach the Faith, we receive divine assistance. It is not we who do the work, but we are the instruments used at that time for the purpose of teaching His Cause."[3]

In another letter, he has explained that:

> "Just one mature soul, with spiritual understanding and a profound knowledge of the Faith, can set a whole country ablaze—so great is the power of the Cause to work through a pure and selfless channel."[4]

As Baháʼís we all try to rid ourselves of ego and strive to be selfless. In this journey towards selflessness, we must realize that it is possible to fall into the trap of self-centeredness even if one's motivations are pure. One can be sincerely interested in the progress and well-being of others, and yet be driven by the desire to be at the center of every situation. In thinking the thought "I help others", a person caught in this trap will place emphasis on "I" and not on "others" or on the act of helping. Try to imagine yourself teaching the Cause to a friend. Which of the following statements would represent your thoughts and feelings if you were consciously trying to avoid self-centeredness? Remember that the absence of self-centeredness does not mean that there is no "self" at all, just that it is not at the center of everything.

_____ May God open his heart and endow him with true understanding.

_____ I hope that my own shortcomings will not prevent her from recognizing the truth of the Faith.

_____ It feels good to teach. I feel great when I convince someone of the truth.

_____ After everything I've done for him, explaining things so carefully, he had better become a Baháʼí.

_____ I hope that my friend will recognize Baháʼu'lláh and feel the same joy that I have felt in serving His Cause.

_____ O God, please put the right thoughts in my mind and give me the right words so that I can teach him properly.

SECTION 4

ʻAbdu'l-Bahá tells us:

> **"Lift up your hearts above the present and look with eyes of faith into the future! Today the seed is sown, the grain falls upon the earth, but behold the day will come when it shall rise a glorious tree and the branches thereof shall be laden with fruit. Rejoice and be glad that this day has dawned, try to realize its power, for it is indeed wonderful! God has crowned you with honor and in your hearts has He set a radiant star; verily the light thereof shall brighten the whole world!"** [5]

The Guardian's advice to us is:

> **"You should, therefore, try all your best to carry aflame within you the torch of faith, for through it you will surely find guidance, strength and eventual success."** [6]

Surely you agree that the reason for someone to enroll in the Baháʼí community is that the spark of faith has been ignited in his or her heart. You would also agree, then, that the teacher of the Cause must be the instrument through which this spark is ignited.

But what if the flame of faith does not burn in the teacher's own heart? With what is he to kindle the spark in his listener's heart? We can set forth the most conclusive proofs and make the most convincing statements, but, without faith, these will have little effect, for the listener can feel whether or not we truly believe in what we say. And the brighter the torch of faith burns in our hearts, the greater the possibility of helping others to recognize Bahá'u'lláh. But in what must the teacher of the Cause have faith? Can you mention a few things? Some examples are given to assist you.

1. <u>Faith in the power of divine assistance.</u>
2. <u>Faith that the Teachings of Bahá'u'lláh are what humanity really needs.</u>
3. <u>Faith in the capacity of every soul to recognize Bahá'u'lláh.</u>
4. _____
5. _____
6. _____
7. _____
8. _____
9. _____
10. _____

SECTION 5

'Abdu'l-Bahá tells us:

> "Speak, therefore; speak out with great courage at every meeting. When thou art about to begin thine address, turn first to Bahá'u'lláh, and ask for the confirmations of the Holy Spirit, then open thy lips and say whatever is suggested to thy heart; this, however, with the utmost courage, dignity and conviction." [7]

And in a letter written on behalf of the Guardian, we read:

> "The Bahá'í teacher must be all confidence. Therein lies his strength and the secret of his success. Though single-handed, and no matter how great the apathy of the people around you may be, you should have faith that the hosts of the Kingdom are on your side, and that through their help you are bound to overcome the forces of darkness that are facing the Cause of God. Persevere, be happy and confident, therefore." [8]

To face new situations, to go to unfamiliar places, to speak to people we hardly know, to share with others that which we consider most precious realizing that it may be rejected takes courage. The source of all courage is, of course, trust in God and reliance on Him. Knowing that He will guide and assist us gives us the strength to do things we would otherwise fear. What happens if we are not courageous when teaching the Cause? Will we lose opportunities? Give some examples of how courage is needed in teaching.

SECTION 6

'Abdu'l-Bahá tells us:

> "The teaching work should under all conditions be actively pursued by the believers because divine confirmations are dependent upon it. Should a Bahá'í refrain from being fully, vigorously and wholeheartedly involved in the teaching work he will undoubtedly be deprived of the blessings of the Abhá Kingdom. Even so, this activity should be tempered with wisdom—not that wisdom which requireth one to be silent and forgetful of such an obligation, but rather that which requireth one to display divine tolerance, love, kindness, patience, a goodly character, and holy deeds." [9]

And in another passage He explains:

> "'Not everything that a man knoweth can be disclosed, nor can everything that he can disclose be regarded as timely, nor can every timely utterance be considered as suited to the capacity of those who hear it.' Such is the consummate wisdom to be observed in thy pursuits. Be not oblivious thereof, if thou wishest to be a man of action under all conditions. First diagnose the disease and identify the malady, then prescribe the remedy, for such is the perfect method of the skillful physician." [10]

Courage must be modified by wisdom. This does not mean that wisdom is supposed to hold back courage. The two should go hand in hand. When a teacher of the Cause has courage and wisdom, he boldly enters the field of action and, with sound judgment and clear thinking, advances. What to say and what not to say, how best to deal with people in a particular situation and how to answer their questions—all these decisions have to be made with wisdom. Wisdom, however, should not become an excuse for inaction. We should not fall into the habit of constantly saying: "It would be unwise to do this. It would be unwise to do that." Below are a few situations in which a teacher of the Cause may find himself or herself. What do you think would be the wisest way to deal with each one?

1. You meet someone at a gathering and enter into a conversation about the Faith. Then he begins to attack the Faith, saying terrible things about the Bahá'í community. What do you do?

2. Someone who seems very interested in the Faith invites you to her home to learn more about it. You present various aspects of the Teachings to her and the visit seems to be going well. She tells you that she likes what she has heard very much and that she thinks the Faith is the answer to humanity's problems. Then she asks you to give her a stack of pamphlets about the Faith so that she can hand them out at the political rally she is attending the next day. What do you do?

3. You are discussing the Faith with two people. As the conversation goes on, it becomes clear that one is interested in the Faith but the other is not. What do you do?

4. You are spending a week in a village participating in a teaching campaign organized jointly by the Area Teaching Committee and the Local Spiritual Assembly. The purpose of the campaign is to increase the number of Bahá'ís by teaching entire families and to consolidate the community. During the day the teachers visit homes and in the evenings, gatherings open to everyone in the village are held, at which various aspects of community life are discussed. To enhance the understanding of the friends, your group presents a skit each night on such themes as the Nineteen Day Feast, Bahá'í children's classes, the Bahá'í wedding ceremony, and Bahá'í burial.

One evening, during consultations on Bahá'í marriage, someone attending the meeting asks you a question. You answer him, but he does not accept your explanation and goes on to express his own views. A few other friends then each address his question, but, after a while, it becomes clear that he is trying to discredit in the eyes of those present the Bahá'í marriage laws. What do you do?

5. You go to a small town with a group of friends to participate in a teaching campaign. After a few days, most of the townspeople come to know that your group is there, and many of them are eager to hear about the Faith. One day, you are walking down the main street with some other friends, when a few men intoxicated with alcohol standing in front of the local bar invite you to come over and explain the Faith to them. What do you do?

SECTION 7

Bahá'u'lláh tells us:

> "Should any one among you be incapable of grasping a certain truth, or be striving to comprehend it, show forth, when conversing with him, a spirit of extreme kindliness and good-will. Help him to see and recognize the truth, without esteeming yourself to be, in the least, superior to him, or to be possessed of greater endowments." [11]

In another passage, He thus exhorts us:

> "Consort with all men, O people of Bahá, in a spirit of friendliness and fellowship. If ye be aware of a certain truth, if ye possess a jewel, of which others are deprived, share it with them in a language of utmost kindliness and good-will. If it be accepted, if it fulfill its purpose, your object is attained. If any one should refuse it, leave him unto himself, and beseech God to guide him. Beware lest ye deal unkindly with him. A kindly tongue is the lodestone of the hearts of men. It is the bread of the spirit, it clotheth the words with meaning, it is the fountain of the light of wisdom and understanding." [12]

As Bahá'ís we strive to show forth loving-kindness and patience in our dealings with people. But we should not confuse kindness with other things. For example, sometimes what appears to be kindness can, in fact, be paternalism. A person who has difficulty recognizing people's capacity and often treats them kindly, but as if they were children, is being paternalistic. Hypocrisy can also present itself as kindness; one can show forth

The Qualities and Attitudes of the Teacher - 47

the utmost loving-kindness, but really have one's own interests in mind. Like kindness, patience can sometimes be misused. For instance, it can be an excuse for negligence. To think about these ideas further, carry out the exercise below.

1. You explain the Faith to someone with great kindness. But when at the end she expresses certain disagreements with you, you become angry. Was your kindness sincere? _____

2. When explaining the Faith to those with less formal education than you, you stop every so often and say: "Do you understand, dear?" Is this kindness or paternalism? _____

3. You are teaching the Faith to someone who is illiterate. You decide that most Bahá'í concepts are too difficult for him to grasp, so you reduce the Message down to a few simple ideas. Is this kindness or paternalism? _____

4. You are teaching the Faith to someone who is illiterate. Although it takes time, you give her a thorough presentation of the Faith, reading with her relevant passages from the Writings and explaining their meaning. Is this patience or paternalism? _____

5. One of your neighbors seems receptive to the Faith, so you decide to teach her. Through a series of discussions and with great kindness, you help her to understand the Teachings and nurture her until she recognizes Bahá'u'lláh. After she has enrolled in the Faith, you continue to nurture her until she herself arises independently to promote the Cause. Is this paternalism? _____

6. You are teaching in a nearby village. After you discuss the Faith with someone for a couple of hours, he tells you that he likes the Teachings and asks you for some literature to read. You give him a small introductory book. Assuming he is semi-illiterate, you decide not to go back and visit him for a few months so that he will have time to read the book. Is this patience or negligence? _____

SECTION 8

Bahá'u'lláh has declared:

> **"If they arise to teach My Cause, they must let the breath of Him Who is the Unconstrained, stir them and must spread it abroad on the earth with high resolve, with minds that are wholly centered in Him, and with hearts that are completely detached from and independent of all things, and with souls that are sanctified from the world and its vanities. It behooveth them to choose as the best provision for their journey reliance upon God, and to clothe themselves with the love of their Lord, the Most Exalted, the All-Glorious. If they do so, their words shall influence their hearers."** [13]

'Abdu'l-Bahá has said:

> "These shall labor ceaselessly, by day and by night, shall heed neither trials nor woe, shall suffer no respite in their efforts, shall seek no repose, shall disregard all ease and comfort, and, detached and unsullied, shall consecrate every fleeting moment of their lives to the diffusion of the divine fragrance and the exaltation of God's holy Word." [14]

We know that detachment is a requirement of joyful teaching. But what does it mean that we should be "detached" when teaching the Cause of God? Completing the sentences below will help you think about this question.

1. When we arise to teach the Cause, we should let the _____ _____ stir us.

2. When we arise to teach the Cause, our minds should be _____ _____.

3. When we arise to teach the Cause, our hearts should be _____ _____, and independent of, _____.

4. When we arise to teach the Cause, our souls should be _____ _____.

5. We should choose as the best provision for our journey _____ _____.

6. We should clothe ourselves with the _____.

7. And having entered the field of service, we should labor _____, by day and by night.

8. We should heed neither _____ nor _____, should seek no _____, and should disregard all _____.

9. Detached and unsullied, we should consecrate _____ _____ of our lives to the _____ _____ and the _____ _____.

The Qualities and Attitudes of the Teacher - 49

SECTION 9

Bahá'u'lláh tells us:

> **"Cry out and summon the people to Him Who is the Sovereign Lord of all the worlds, with such zeal and fervor that all men may be set on fire by thee."** [15]

Shoghi Effendi tells us:

> **". . . let us arise to teach His Cause with righteousness, conviction, understanding and vigor. Let this be the paramount and most urgent duty of every Bahá'í. Let us make it the dominating passion of our life."** [16]

If we are to succeed in our efforts to win over large numbers to the Cause, we must be driven by a passion to teach the Faith. Our hearts must be fired by enthusiasm, for how are we to convey the joy of being a Bahá'í, if we are not ourselves joyful and enthusiastic? But in our eagerness to share Bahá'u'lláh's Message with others, we should take care not to overstep proper bounds and turn away those whom we seek to teach. A word one often hears in this connection is "proselytization", which means to put undue pressure on someone to change his Faith. Bahá'ís are strictly forbidden to proselytize. Yet, in avoiding proselytization, we should not be so passive and so unconvincing that our teaching efforts have no effect.

To help you think about the difference between passion in teaching and proselytization, read the following statements and decide in which cases you would be overstepping proper bounds. Mark them with an "O". In which would you be so unenthusiastic that you would be ineffective? Mark them with a "U". In which cases would your approach be enthusiastic and within proper limits? Mark them with an "E".

- **E**   You are so enamored with the Faith that at every opportunity you introduce into your conversations, in a natural way and with wisdom, Bahá'í principles and teachings. When appropriate, you mention the source of your ideas as the teachings of Bahá'u'lláh.

- **O**   You are so enthusiastic that even if people do not want to listen to your presentation about the Faith, you practically force them to.

- **E**   You are so enamored with the Faith that whenever you talk to people, you always manage to change the conversation and to bring it around to Bahá'u'lláh and His Teachings.

- **U**   You don't want people to think you're fanatical about your religion, so even if they ask you about the Faith, you only give a short answer. If they persist and ask again, then you finally give them a book and tell them to read it for themselves.

- **E**   You wish to open a neighboring town to the Faith and go off to spend the afternoon there. You know that it is culturally unacceptable to the people of the town for a stranger to knock on their doors and talk about religion. But you decide you must have faith, say a prayer, and start going from house to house.

__E__   You wish to open a neighboring town to the Faith and go off to spend the afternoon there. You know that it is culturally unacceptable to the people of the town for a stranger to knock on their doors and talk about religion. So you decide that all you can do there is to say some prayers and then go home.

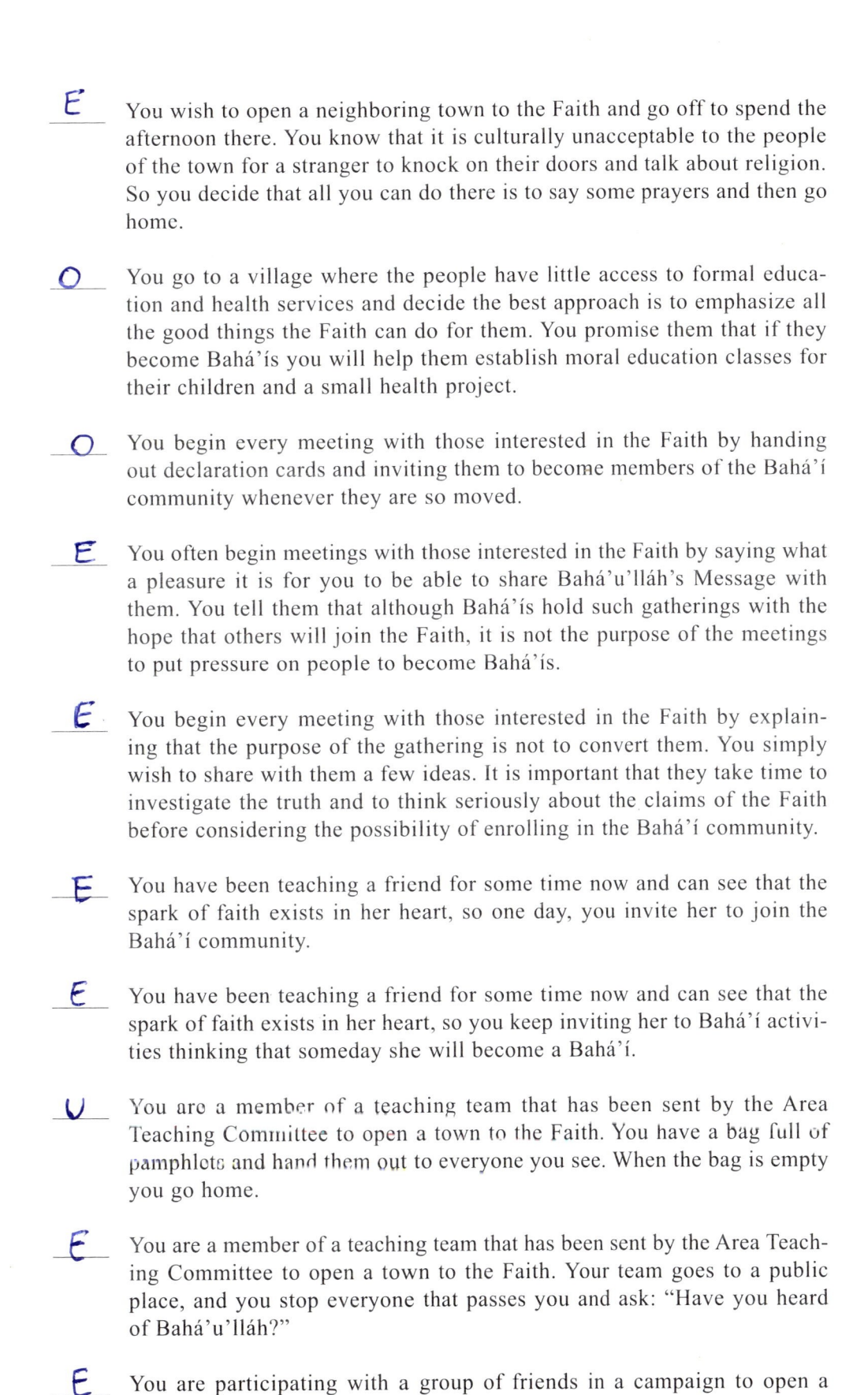

__O__   You go to a village where the people have little access to formal education and health services and decide the best approach is to emphasize all the good things the Faith can do for them. You promise them that if they become Bahá'ís you will help them establish moral education classes for their children and a small health project.

__O__   You begin every meeting with those interested in the Faith by handing out declaration cards and inviting them to become members of the Bahá'í community whenever they are so moved.

__E__   You often begin meetings with those interested in the Faith by saying what a pleasure it is for you to be able to share Bahá'u'lláh's Message with them. You tell them that although Bahá'ís hold such gatherings with the hope that others will join the Faith, it is not the purpose of the meetings to put pressure on people to become Bahá'ís.

__E__   You begin every meeting with those interested in the Faith by explaining that the purpose of the gathering is not to convert them. You simply wish to share with them a few ideas. It is important that they take time to investigate the truth and to think seriously about the claims of the Faith before considering the possibility of enrolling in the Bahá'í community.

__E__   You have been teaching a friend for some time now and can see that the spark of faith exists in her heart, so one day, you invite her to join the Bahá'í community.

__E__   You have been teaching a friend for some time now and can see that the spark of faith exists in her heart, so you keep inviting her to Bahá'í activities thinking that someday she will become a Bahá'í.

__U__   You are a member of a teaching team that has been sent by the Area Teaching Committee to open a town to the Faith. You have a bag full of pamphlets and hand them out to everyone you see. When the bag is empty you go home.

__E__   You are a member of a teaching team that has been sent by the Area Teaching Committee to open a town to the Faith. Your team goes to a public place, and you stop everyone that passes you and ask: "Have you heard of Bahá'u'lláh?"

__E__   You are participating with a group of friends in a campaign to open a neighboring town. The plan is to go to the public park and sit and pray for long hours, with the hope that people will be attracted to you, will come to you, and then you will be able to teach them.

The Qualities and Attitudes of the Teacher - 51

___E___ You are participating with a group of friends in a campaign to open a neighboring town. When you arrive in the town, you and a few other members of the group set up a small exhibition with books and photographs near the market, after receiving permission from the local authorities. The idea is for each of you to take turns sitting near the exhibition booth. People will pass by and stop to look at the literature and pictures. If they express interest in the Faith by asking a question or making some comments you are to speak to them.

___E___ You are participating in a campaign to open a neighboring town where previous efforts to teach have not been effective. As part of the initial phase of the campaign your group has studied the town well and become familiar with the various organizations, the educational and social establishments, and the programs promoting social progress. You have also collected from other believers the names of a few people in the town who may be receptive to the Faith. On the basis of all this information, your group devises a plan with a range of activities which include interviews at the local radio station, exhibitions in a few public places, and visits to the local authorities, schools and other organizations. Through one of your contacts, for example, arrangements are made to give a presentation at the secondary school and to a women's group. As you meet people, you draw up a list of those you will invite to coffee or lunch or to meetings that are held during the evenings. You have also prepared a weekend workshop on the theme "The Implications of Spirituality for Humanity Today" and invite interested people to attend. Since one of the members of your group is particularly good at meeting people in public places—something he does in a very natural and inoffensive way—he spends much of his time inviting people to the various activities you are carrying out.

___E___ Your Area Teaching Committee has organized a campaign to teach in a number of villages where the people are very open and receptive. Your team decides that the best approach is to go from house to house and introduce the Faith as, in fact, most people would be upset if you visited a neighbor and did not visit them.

SECTION 10

As mentioned earlier, the emphasis we have placed on spiritual qualities in our discussion of teaching does not imply that the teacher of the Cause is expected to be perfect. What is required is to set a goal and to work conscientiously towards it. One must be willing to walk the path towards perfection no matter how far off the final goal may appear. And it is essential to remember that to walk this path, one must possess humility. For without humility, success becomes the cause of downfall, and the seeds that one sows in the hearts of others become contaminated. 'Abdu'l-Bahá tells us:

"The teacher, when teaching, must be himself fully enkindled, so that his utterance, like unto a flame of fire, may exert influence and consume the veil

of self and passion. He must also be utterly humble and lowly so that others may be edified, and be totally self-effaced and evanescent so that he may teach with the melody of the Concourse on high—otherwise his teaching will have no effect." [17]

And in another passage He cautions us:

> "In accordance with the divine teachings in this glorious dispensation we should not belittle anyone and call him ignorant, saying: 'You know not, but I know.' Rather, we should look upon others with respect, and when attempting to explain and demonstrate, we should speak as if we are investigating the truth, saying: 'Here these things are before us. Let us investigate to determine where and in what form the truth can be found.' The teacher should not consider himself as learned and others ignorant. Such a thought breedeth pride, and pride is not conducive to influence. The teacher should not see in himself any superiority; he should speak with the utmost kindliness, lowliness and humility, for such speech exerteth influence and educateth the souls." [18]

1. What is the difference between the passion referred to in the first quotation and the passion discussed in the preceding section? _____

2. Can you give a few examples of how humility increases the influence exerted by our words? _____

SECTION 11

There is another point related to humility that deserves our attention as we explore the question of teaching. It is true that we must constantly strive to improve our inner condition and develop those qualities that will help us become increasingly effective teachers of the Cause. Yet, while consciously working to perfect our characters, we should never let the thought creep into our minds that our success in the teaching field is the result of our own merits. Humility will protect us from gaining a feeling of self-importance.

We must always separate our accomplishments in teaching from ourselves. Any part we play in helping a soul to recognize Bahá'u'lláh is a gift bestowed upon us by God. He chooses those through whom He will work. We can only hope to become a channel through which He operates and strive to acquire those qualities that will enable us to become His instruments. The following passage from a letter written on behalf of Shoghi Effendi provides us with a warning:

> **"Perhaps the reason why you have not accomplished so much in the field of teaching is the extent you looked upon your own weaknesses and inabilities to spread the Message. Bahá'u'lláh and the Master have both urged us repeatedly to disregard our own handicaps and lay our whole reliance upon God. He will come to our help if we only arise and become an active channel for God's grace. Do you think it is the teachers who make converts and change human hearts? No, surely not. They are only pure souls who take the first step, and then let the spirit of Bahá'u'lláh move them and make use of them. If any one of them should even for a second consider his achievements as due to his own capacities, his work is ended and his fall starts. This is in fact the reason why so many competent souls have after wonderful services suddenly found themselves absolutely impotent and perhaps thrown aside by the Spirit of the Cause as useless souls. The criterion is the extent to which we are ready to have the will of God operate through us.**
>
> **"Stop being conscious of your frailties, therefore; have a perfect reliance upon God; let your heart burn with the desire to serve His mission and proclaim His call; and you will observe how eloquence and the power to change human hearts will come as a matter of course.**
>
> **"Shoghi Effendi will surely pray for your success if you should arise and start to teach. In fact the mere act of arising will win for you God's help and blessings."** [19]

1. Can you give a few examples of how pride and arrogance make an otherwise accomplished teacher of the Cause ineffective? _____

    _____
    _____
    _____
    _____
    _____
    _____
    _____

2. Humility is not only essential in the act of teaching. When pride creeps into our actions, it eventually makes us ineffective in any field of service. To think about the different forms pride can take in relation to teaching, carry out the following exercise:

A teaching project with highly successful methods and approaches is underway in a particular region of the country. One of the friends feels, however, that the project does not use what he considers to be his most outstanding talents. Which of the following reactions shows a lack of pride on his part?

_____ Refusing to participate in the project because it does not allow him to use his talents as he wishes.

_____ Participating joyfully in the project, working along side his fellow believers in whatever way is necessary and drawing upon his other capacities.

_____ Trying to find fault with the project, saying that it is really not a good project because it does not draw upon all the talents and capacities of the friends.

A Bahá'í community is exploring different approaches to teaching in order to accelerate the growth of the Faith. Some of the members of the community hear about an approach being used in another area that is bringing excellent results. Which of the following would be the most appropriate response, reflecting neither pride nor lack of wisdom?

_____ Concluding, without examining the approach, that it could not possibly work in their city since it was designed by others somewhere else.

_____ Concluding that if the approach worked in one place, it should work in another and should be adopted without change.

_____ Examining the approach carefully to see if all or part of it could work in a new setting and, on that basis, adopting the approach and then modifying it in whatever way experience shows is necessary.

A traveling teacher visits a community which he does not know, and a meeting is arranged for him to speak to a group of Bahá'ís. Which of the following actions shows a lack of pride on the part of the traveling teacher?

_____ Giving a simplified introduction to the Faith, assuming that the people know little.

_____ Seeking guidance from the Local Spiritual Assembly, or the committee in charge, to find out the level of knowledge and experience of those who will be present and, on that basis, choosing an appropriate subject for the meeting.

_____ Deciding that since all Bahá'ís need encouragement, they should hear a fiery talk urging them to be more active and sacrificial—this, in spite of the fact that, unknown to him, most of those present are highly active in the Faith.

One of the believers has been asked by the National Teaching Committee to visit a group teaching in a certain region of the country. The group has actually been doing quite well, and its efforts to help expand and consolidate the local communities are beginning to bear fruit. Which of the following reflects a sense of humility on the part of the visiting believer?

_____ Listening to what the group has to say about their experience, participating with them in action, offering suggestions when needed, finding out how the Committee can help them, and taking a full report back to the Committee so that their experience might be shared with others.

_____ Making it clear that he has been sent by the Committee, therefore, giving the group a long list of instructions to follow.

_____ Taking the opportunity to practice his leadership qualities and giving the group a speech on the dynamics of heroic action.

A regional teaching campaign is soon to get under way, and all the participants have been divided into groups, each one with a coordinator. When the groups meet to discuss their plans, one of the friends finds that the coordinator of his group is a believer to whom he had himself taught the Faith. Which of the following shows a lack of pride on his part?

_____ Trying to take control of the group by ignoring the coordinator and telling her what to do in front of the others.

_____ Refusing to join the group unless someone more experienced, like himself, is named the coordinator.

_____ Feeling great happiness at seeing the progress this believer has made and joining the team with joy, working hard to contribute his share to its success.

SECTION 12

In the previous sections we have examined humility in two ways, as a quality that endows our speech with influence, and as protection against the pitfalls lying in the path of spiritual progress. There is yet another significant contribution humility makes to our lives that is specially relevant to teaching. Humility allows us to approach life with an attitude of learning. In the absence of such an attitude we tend to become blind to our own ignorance and believe we know that which we do not know. A most praiseworthy characteristic of those who walk humbly with their Lord is their willingness to learn.

Why, we may ask, is having a positive attitude towards learning so important for those of us who wish to become effective teachers of the Cause? In order to answer this question, reflect on what you know about teaching. Do you always know the most appropriate method of teaching to use? Do you know what to say and how to say it in every situation that presents itself to you? Do you think it is possible to learn in a course or two all that you need to know about approaches to teaching? Is there a formula that can be presented to you? Surely you agree that the answer to these questions is "no" and that the only reasonable way to go about improving one's teaching methods is to adopt a posture of learning.

As you strive to become a better and better teacher of the Cause you should be careful not to fall into the trap of arguing with your fellow believers over teaching methods. If not careful, we can easily become engaged in this kind of argument, each of us believing that we have found the right formula and that, unless teaching is done our way, success is impossible.

We avoid such behavior when we decide that becoming an effective teacher of the Cause is something that has to be learned. We free ourselves of self-imposed limitations when we see in every teaching effort an opportunity to acquire insights and improve our approaches and methods. Our conversations with our Bahá'í friends are most fruitful when we exchange ideas, share teaching experiences and analyze the causes of success.

Read the situations presented below. How would you respond to each one if you were determined to see in every teaching effort an opportunity to learn?

1. One summer you go travel-teaching to a region where the culture of the people is very different from your own. You use the same presentation of the Faith that has proved successful at home. But, here, it does not bring any results. You decide:

   _____ The people are not receptive and you should go somewhere else.

   _____ You need to come up with a new presentation that will be better understood by the local people and will touch their hearts.

   _____ You should continue giving your presentation as you always have, for perseverance is the most important quality of a teacher.

   _____ You are being punished by God for your shortcomings, and you should work on your own spiritual development before taking any more teaching trips.

2. As part of your own personal teaching plan, you decide to hold a weekly meeting at your home to discuss the Faith. You invite about ten people who have, on different occasions, expressed interest. For each meeting, you choose some subject and prepare and deliver a short talk on it, following which you open the meeting for questions. You then have a period of hospitality in which you socialize and sing songs. After a few weeks, only two people are still coming. You decide:

   _____ You need to make the meetings more entertaining and social.

   _____ You should drop the weekly meetings from your teaching plan; it wasn't such a good idea after all.

   _____ You should try a different format in the next few meetings, perhaps studying a short selection of quotations from the Writings on a particular subject together with your guests, allowing them to become familiar with the Holy Word, and build on that experience.

   _____ You should seek out all the people who are not coming any longer and ask them why they stopped attending the meetings.

The Qualities and Attitudes of the Teacher - 57

3. When you were learning about the Faith, there were a few principles that struck you most: the unity of humankind, the elimination of every form of prejudice, and universal education. So now you feel that the best way to teach people is to present these same principles to them. While in general everyone to whom you speak is in agreement with the ideas you express, no one becomes particularly interested in the Faith. You decide:

_____ You need more practice in presenting the principles.

_____ You should seek out people like yourself and only teach them.

_____ You are not a natural-born teacher and you should serve the Faith in some other way.

_____ You should discuss your experience with a few Bahá'ís to find other ways of introducing the Faith to people.

4. You are a new Bahá'í and have heard much about the importance of teaching since joining the community. So one day you determine to draw up a personal teaching plan. Because you have never done this before, you consult with a few more experienced believers, and they present you with numerous ideas about how to teach the Faith. You decide:

_____ You will make a list of all the ideas and, starting from the top, will try each one.

_____ You will take the approach of one of the friends whose ideas promise a great deal of excitement and glamour.

_____ There are so many ways to go about teaching that it is best not to make a plan, but to teach as the spirit moves you.

_____ You will think about all the ideas and, on the basis of those most suited to your situation, decide on a few steps to take. You will then carry out these steps. As you reflect on what you are doing, questions will arise in your mind and you will turn to the writings to find answers to them. In the light of the insights you gain from experience and the passages you study, you will determine what next few steps to take. You will repeat this pattern again and again.

5. As part of your personal teaching plan, you have decided to focus your efforts on a particular population and share Bahá'u'lláh's Message with them. After a while you notice from the questions they ask that they all seem to have difficulty accepting the existence of God. You decide:

_____ It is better not to talk about this subject. If they bring it up in your discussions, you will quickly move on to another topic.

_____ It is impossible to teach a people that has difficulty with the concept of God, so you will choose a new group on which to focus your energies.

_____ You will ask a more experienced teacher to visit them with you and give a talk to them about the existence of God. If that does not work, then you will leave them and insist no longer.

_____ After studying some of the relevant passages from the writings, you will prepare a short statement in your own words to explain to them what Bahá'u'lláh teaches about God. You will listen to their reactions, reflect on the results, go back to the writings to find answers to the questions raised, and modify your statement in the light of the insights you gain from experience and the passages you study. You will continue doing this until your explanation begins to bring satisfactory results.

6. You had the bounty of participating in a highly successful one-month teaching campaign in a village near your home. Knowing how important it is to deepen the newly enrolled believers, the Area Teaching Committee assigns you several families to visit regularly. For your first visit you do not prepare any materials, thinking you will say whatever comes to your mind. But you end up simply repeating the introductory presentation that you gave when they enrolled in the Faith. Realizing if you do this forever, nothing will be achieved, you decide:

_____ You will prepare a list of thirty talks on a wide range of subjects and will present a new subject to them each visit, following your list faithfully to ensure you cover all the topics you have chosen.

_____ You will give each family a small booklet about the Faith and ask them to read a certain number of pages in between your visits. During your visits, then, you will discuss with them any questions they have.

_____ This approach is impractical and time-consuming. Instead of visiting the families one by one, you will invite them to a weekly meeting at someone's home to discuss the Faith. "Those that are really interested in learning will come," you tell yourself.

_____ You will think of one basic idea that you feel would be helpful for them to learn and will find relevant passages on the subject in the writings to present to them. You will visit one of the families and share with it the passages and discuss the ideas. You will reflect on the results of the meeting, go back to the writings, modify the selection of passages and use them for a visit to another family. Meanwhile, in the light of the comments made during the visit to the first family, you will choose another set of ideas and passages to study with it during your second visit. You will continue this process until you have a pattern of visits with a theme for each one.

SECTION 13

One of the challenges before Bahá'ís today is to learn how to sustain the large-scale expansion and consolidation of their communities. Some time ago, mostly during the 1960s and 1970s, numerous teaching projects conducted with great enthusiasm around the world brought thousands upon thousands into the Faith. But, because we were not able to deepen Bahá'ís in large numbers, the expansion process eventually slowed down and in many places came to a halt. In 1996 the Universal House of Justice launched the Four Year Plan and called on the worldwide Bahá'í community to make a significant advance in the process of entry by troops. Now Bahá'ís everywhere are once again focused on large-scale expansion and consolidation and, with the establishment of a growing number of institutes to train ever-increasing contingents of believers in acts of service, are approaching this task in a posture of learning. Clearly this is a challenge the Bahá'í world will face for decades to come.

To think about how to approach expansion and consolidation with an attitude of learning, imagine yourself in the following situation which, although somewhat artificial, draws from real experience of the past.

You are a member of a group of believers teaching in a highly receptive region of the country. You are amazed by the openness of the people and how readily they accept Bahá'u'lláh and enroll in the Faith. You decide that the time is ripe, and you should concentrate all your efforts on bringing large numbers into the Faith. Consolidation can be dealt with later. And so you move from village to village and in the course of a few months enroll several thousand individuals. Your group is filled with joy. But when, after several months, you go back to visit the new Bahá'ís, you find that the initial enthusiasm is gone, and there is little response to your efforts to foster Bahá'í community life.

Your group consults about what to do next. You look into the writings and read the guidance of the Universal House of Justice which states that expansion and consolidation are "twin processes that must go hand in hand." [20] After much deliberation, you decide that since the expansion process has raced ahead of consolidation, you should now focus your efforts on deepening the newly enrolled believers. You feel that this should also be done on a large-scale and conclude that slide shows are the answer. So the group designs a series of slide shows and takes them from village to village, holding large meetings with the friends. Months pass, and the meetings always attract an enthusiastic audience. But when the series ends, and you go back to the villages without the slides, everyone is disappointed. You discover that the believers actually learned very little through the slide presentations, and the number of those attending the community meetings gradually decreases. When elections for the Local Spiritual Assemblies are held at Riḍván, only a few show up in each village.

This same pattern occurs everywhere. However, in one village there is a family that has developed a strong Bahá'í identity and, because of its presence, the community seems to be doing better than the others. Meetings held in the home of this family are joyful and effective. The daughter, an energetic fourteen year old, has joined a teaching team and is also starting to hold Bahá'í children's classes. Your group consults with the Area Teaching Committee, and it is decided that you should try to raise up one strong family in each village.

The group breaks into teams of two, and each is assigned a family in one village to visit regularly over a period of several months and deepen in the Faith. These families always look forward to your visits, and you spend many happy hours together. But, in general, things do not go as expected, and you discover that concentrating all your efforts on a single family has many drawbacks. Rather than the families becoming a stimulus for Bahá'í activity, most of them have become a barrier to growth. Receiving your visits makes them feel special, and they use this to show off to their neighbors. In fact, many are kept back from approaching you by the families themselves who are reluctant to share your friendship with others. What should you do next, you ask yourselves.

The group again consults with the Area Teaching Committee, turning to the writings for an answer to the many questions that have arisen. Expansion in the area has nearly come to a stop, and your efforts to consolidate the communities and deepen the new believers have met with little success. You spend long hours deliberating and decide that the key lies in the strengthening and development of the Local Spiritual Assemblies. After all, the Universal House of Justice has said that "success in this one goal will greatly enrich the quality of Bahá'í life" and will "heighten the capacity of the Faith to deal with entry by troops".[21] Teams once again go off to the villages, this time with the aim of deepening the nine members of each Assembly, confident that if these develop a strong Bahá'í identity, the Local Assemblies will begin to function properly and the problems of consolidation will be solved.

But at the end of a year of persistent effort, you realize your strategy is not working. Community life does not exist, and the Local Spiritual Assemblies are not taking up the affairs of the Faith. In fact, at this stage of development, it is clear that many of the Local Spiritual Assembly members are not the most enthusiastic believers in the communities, and unfortunately, some of them are not interested much in learning about the Faith. You realize that by concentrating on only these nine, you are neglecting a number of capable believers who would respond to your deepening efforts. At Riḍván, most of the members of the Assemblies change, and you are not sure anymore if it is worth focusing once again on the nine new members, to the exclusion of others.

Of course, your work has not been in vain during all this time. Strong and steadfast believers have arisen in each community. Some communities have reached a stage where they undertake activities once in a while, and a few Local Assemblies meet, but only when someone from outside visits them. Decide which of the following should occur at this point:

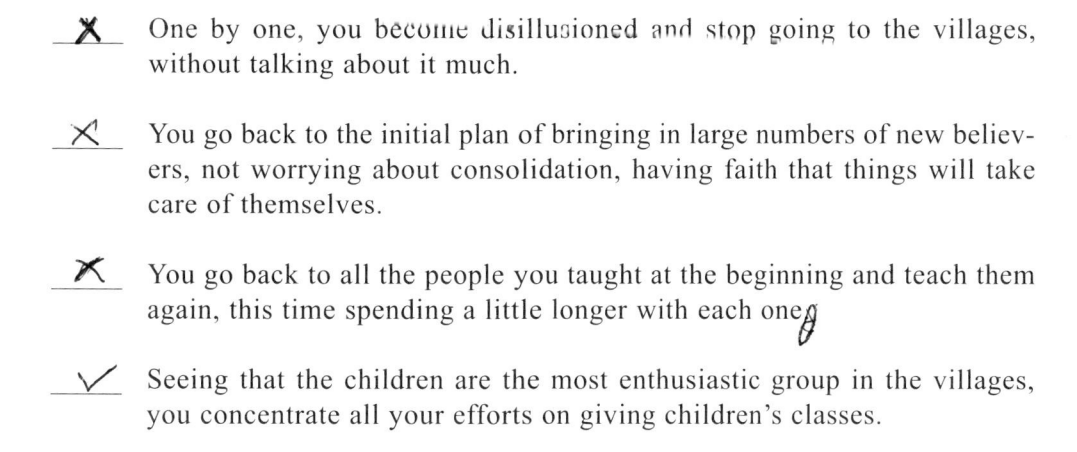

    __X__   One by one, you become disillusioned and stop going to the villages, without talking about it much.

    __X__   You go back to the initial plan of bringing in large numbers of new believers, not worrying about consolidation, having faith that things will take care of themselves.

    __X__   You go back to all the people you taught at the beginning and teach them again, this time spending a little longer with each one.

    __✓__   Seeing that the children are the most enthusiastic group in the villages, you concentrate all your efforts on giving children's classes.

_X_   Given that the Local Spiritual Assembly by itself, without community life, does not work, you now concentrate all your efforts on getting the Nineteen Day Feast established.

_✓_   Since the people need to read the Word of God by themselves, you launch a literacy campaign and focus all your energies on that.

You probably feel that none of the courses of action mentioned above is adequate by itself. So let us assume that the Area Teaching Committee calls a meeting of the more active believers in the region, who now include a number of friends from the villages themselves, for a few days of consultation on a plan of action that would bring about the sustained, accelerated growth of the Faith. Discuss this with your group. Although you cannot devise a plan without being in a real situation, write down as many of the elements as you can imagine would be included in an effective plan of action:

Ruhi study cycles – children classes – Devotional Gathering. Identifying key individual.

SECTION 14

There are two sources from which we can learn how to teach effectively. One is the writings of the Faith and the other is experience, our own and that of our fellow believers. The way we go about learning, then, must include both the study of the writings and the accumulation of experience. We should have a systematic plan of personal teaching and follow it. We should also contribute to the projects designed or promoted by our institutions and collaborate with others in the systematic expansion and consolidation of the Faith within a receptive population.

As we teach we should reflect on what we have done, on the effectiveness of what we have said and how we have said it. Continual action and reflection will give rise to important questions which we should try to answer by studying relevant passages from the Bahá'í writings. This study of the writings we need not carry out alone. We can hold meetings of consultation with other Bahá'í friends, search the writings together and share the insights we gain from experience, from reflection, and from study. Following a pattern of action and reflection in the light of Bahá'u'lláh's Revelation is, of course, an absolute necessity when we are collectively engaged in organized teaching campaigns. If we fail to do so, we run the danger of entering into arguments over teaching methods and, after much discussion—each of us defending the method he or she thinks is best—deciding to follow one method or another half-heartedly. Unfortunately, if this happens often, we all end up feeling lukewarm about teaching.

SECTION 15

One set of questions that will emerge time and again as we pursue the above-mentioned pattern of consultation, action and reflection has to do with the way we approach teaching and the attitudes we adopt in carrying out this sacred duty. Should we be very bold? Should we be cautious and conservative? Should we give the Message immediately to every person we meet or should we be selective? Should we talk directly about the Faith as the religion for humanity today, or should we limit our conversations to a general discussion of principles that are easily acceptable to people? Should we mention those aspects of the Teachings that we know will be challenging to the listener, or should we leave all such subjects for later, after the person has accepted the Faith? In order to be convincing, should we make our presentations strong and overwhelming, or should we speak with as little passion as possible?

In the passage below, the Guardian gives us invaluable advice in this respect. You may not know the meaning of some of the words, so before studying the quotation, review the following list of definitions:

Provocative:	Causing anger or strong disagreement
Supine:	Laid back
Fanatical:	Filled with excessive or mistaken enthusiasm
Excessive:	Beyond what is normal or proper
Liberal:	Broad-minded; not bound by tradition or rules
Exposition:	An explanation of meaning or purpose; presentation of a theme
Wary:	Cautious
Conciliatory:	Willing to give in
Layman:	A person who is not a clergyman
Contemptuous:	Showing disrespect or disdain; scornful
Whittle down:	Reduce bit by bit
Proffer:	To present for acceptance; to offer
Uncompromising:	Not making or allowing a comprise; unyielding; immovable

Now read the quotation from the writings of the Guardian:

"They must be neither provocative nor supine, neither fanatical nor excessively liberal, in their exposition of the fundamental and distinguishing features of their Faith. They must be either wary or bold, they must act swiftly or mark time, they must use the direct or indirect method, they must be challenging

or conciliatory, in strict accordance with the spiritual receptivity of the soul with whom they come in contact, whether he be a nobleman or a commoner, a northerner or a southerner, a layman or a priest, a capitalist or a socialist, a statesman or a prince, an artisan or a beggar. In their presentation of the Message of Bahá'u'lláh they must neither hesitate nor falter. They must be neither contemptuous of the poor nor timid before the great. In their exposition of its verities they must neither overstress nor whittle down the truth which they champion, whether their hearer belong to royalty, or be a prince of the church, or a politician, or a tradesman, or a man of the street. To all alike, high or low, rich or poor, they must proffer, with open hands, with a radiant heart, with an eloquent tongue, with infinite patience, with uncompromising loyalty, with great wisdom, with unshakable courage, the Cup of Salvation at so critical an hour . . ." [22]

1. Shoghi Effendi tells us that when teaching the Cause, we must be neither _____ Provocative _____ nor _____ in our _____ of the _____ and _____ features of the Faith.

2. Nor must we be _____ or _____ in our exposition.

3. We must be either _____ or _____, we must act _____ or _____, we must use the _____ or _____ method, we must be _____ or _____, in strict accordance with the _____ of the soul with whom we come in contact.

4. When teaching the Cause, we must act in strict _____ with the _____ of the soul with whom we come in contact, whether he be a nobleman or a _____, a northerner or a _____, a layman or a _____, a capitalist or a _____, a statesman or a _____, an artisan or a _____.

5. We must be neither _____ of the poor nor _____ before the great.

6. In our exposition of the verities of the Faith, we must neither _____ nor _____ the truth which we champion, whether our hearer belong to _____, or be a _____

64 - The Qualities and Attitudes of the Teacher

_____, or a _____, or a _____,
or a _____.

7. To all alike, _____ or _____, _____ or _____, we must proffer, with _____ hands, with a _____ heart, with an _____ tongue, with _____ patience, with _____ loyalty, with _____ wisdom, with _____ courage, the Cup of Salvation at this critical hour.

SECTION 16

Now let us examine the above quotation more closely and try to discover some of its practical implications.

1. The quotation tells us that when we teach the Cause, we should not be provocative in our presentation. Below are a few situations. Put a "P" next to those in which your presentation is provocative.

    P   In order to demonstrate to a devout believer in another Faith that humanity is in need of a new Manifestation, you begin your presentation by drawing his attention to all the things that have gone wrong with his religion.

    _____ You explain to a devout believer in another Faith that the Manifestations of God are like mirrors reflecting the light of the sun. They reflect the qualities of God and reveal His divine attributes. Though the Mirrors may differ, They all reflect the Light of the same Sun. In this way, you help him gradually come to understand that accepting Bahá'u'lláh does not mean rejecting the Manifestations that came before Him.

    P   You are teaching someone who is not sure whether she believes in God. You begin by telling her that Bahá'u'lláh is the Supreme Manifestation of God.

    P   A small group has gathered at your home. Most of those present have as yet shown little interest in the Faith and you are only trying to introduce the Teachings to them. During the course of your discussions you state emphatically that, in the future, everyone is going to become Bahá'í.

    P   You begin your presentation to someone who has all the comforts of life by saying that wealth is a veil between a person and God.

    P   You meet a clergyman who is genuinely interested in learning about the Faith and asks you to explain some of the Teachings of Bahá'u'lláh to him. The first thing you tell him is that, in this Age, God has abolished the priesthood.

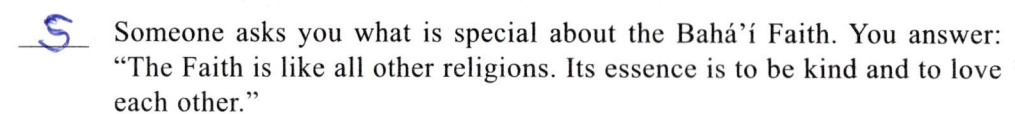

2. When we teach the Cause, we should not be supine. In which of the following situations are you too laid back? Mark them with an "S".

   S Someone asks you what is special about the Bahá'í Faith. You answer: "The Faith is like all other religions. Its essence is to be kind and to love each other."

   S Your method of teaching others is to try to show them that the Faith is a collection of noble principles which anyone can accept. "The establishment of peace," you say, for example, "who doesn't believe in that?" Once they become attracted to the Faith in this way, you leave them to themselves, sometimes telling them that they can have a book to read if they wish. That is as far as you ever go.

   S Someone close to accepting the Faith asks you about finances and contributions. Your entire answer is: "Sure, like everything else in life, some money is needed to do things. But you will contribute only if you want to."

   _____ Someone close to accepting the Faith asks you about finances and contributions. You tell him that contributing to the funds of the Faith is the sacred obligation of every believer and explain to him the spiritual significance of sacrifice, which implies giving up that which is lower to receive that which is higher. "Contributing to the funds", you say, "is an integral part of our work to build a better world."

   S A friend who has been studying the Faith for some time asks you to explain the concept of the Eternal Covenant to him. You say that it is really very simple: "There is an agreement between God and man. From time to time, He sends His Manifestation, and we recognize Him and try our best to do what He says."

3. When we teach the Cause, we should not be fanatical in our presentation. Below are several situations. Put an "F" next to those in which your presentation is fanatical.

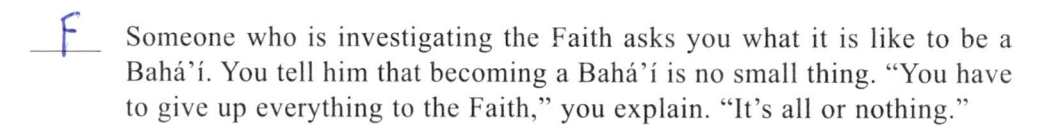

   F Someone who is investigating the Faith asks you what it is like to be a Bahá'í. You tell him that becoming a Bahá'í is no small thing. "You have to give up everything to the Faith," you explain. "It's all or nothing."

   F You begin a meeting at your home with group of people who have come for the first time to hear about the Faith by asking them to hold hands in a circle and sing "Alláh-u-Abhá".

   F You begin teaching a devout believer in another faith by telling her that the time of her religion is over and done with. She should abandon her religion. "Bahá'u'lláh, the Messenger of God for today, has come," you tell her. "You should throw away the past."

66 - The Qualities and Attitudes of the Teacher

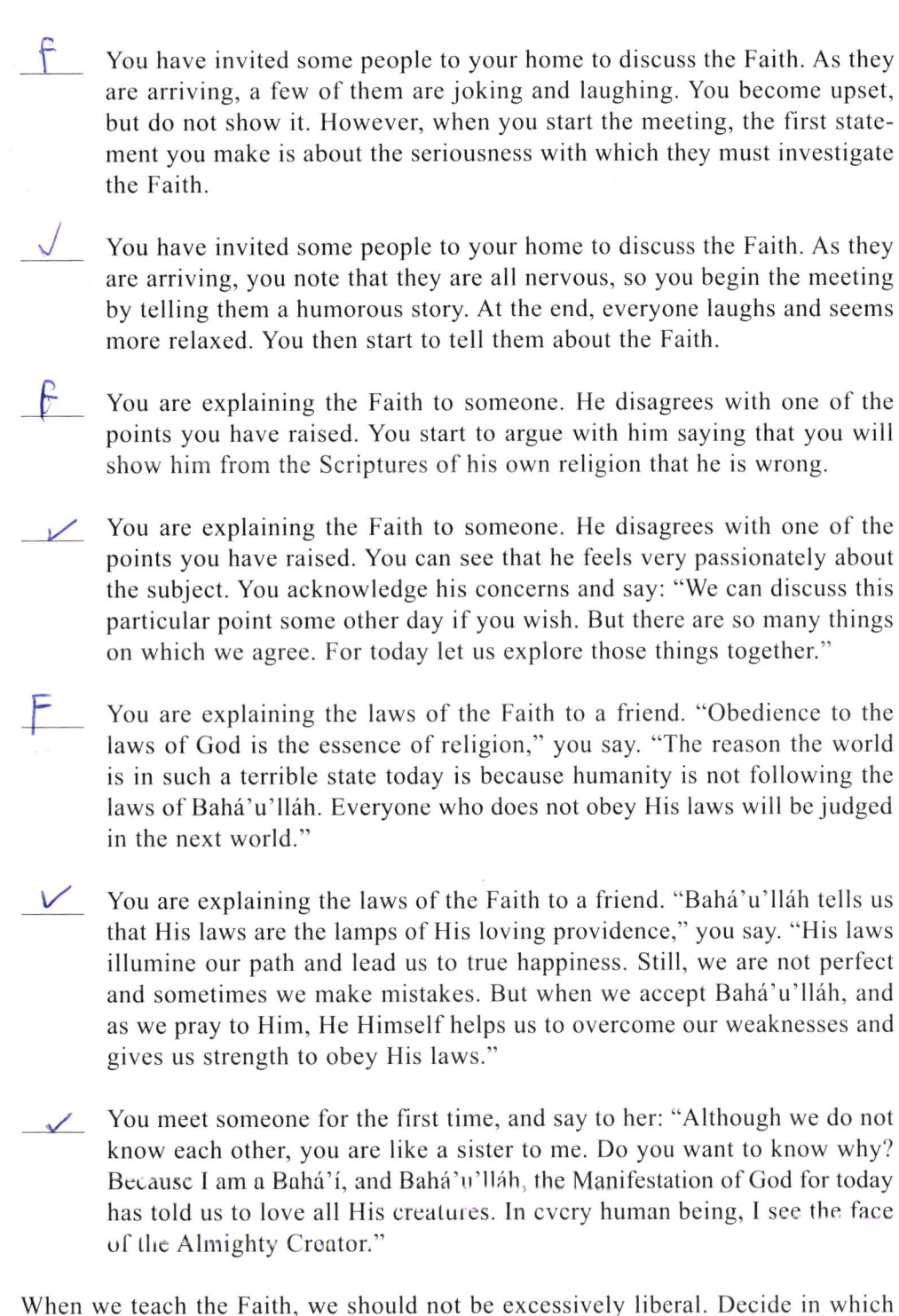

___F___ You have invited some people to your home to discuss the Faith. As they are arriving, a few of them are joking and laughing. You become upset, but do not show it. However, when you start the meeting, the first statement you make is about the seriousness with which they must investigate the Faith.

___✓___ You have invited some people to your home to discuss the Faith. As they are arriving, you note that they are all nervous, so you begin the meeting by telling them a humorous story. At the end, everyone laughs and seems more relaxed. You then start to tell them about the Faith.

___F___ You are explaining the Faith to someone. He disagrees with one of the points you have raised. You start to argue with him saying that you will show him from the Scriptures of his own religion that he is wrong.

___✓___ You are explaining the Faith to someone. He disagrees with one of the points you have raised. You can see that he feels very passionately about the subject. You acknowledge his concerns and say: "We can discuss this particular point some other day if you wish. But there are so many things on which we agree. For today let us explore those things together."

___F___ You are explaining the laws of the Faith to a friend. "Obedience to the laws of God is the essence of religion," you say. "The reason the world is in such a terrible state today is because humanity is not following the laws of Bahá'u'lláh. Everyone who does not obey His laws will be judged in the next world."

___✓___ You are explaining the laws of the Faith to a friend. "Bahá'u'lláh tells us that His laws are the lamps of His loving providence," you say. "His laws illumine our path and lead us to true happiness. Still, we are not perfect and sometimes we make mistakes. But when we accept Bahá'u'lláh, and as we pray to Him, He Himself helps us to overcome our weaknesses and gives us strength to obey His laws."

___✓___ You meet someone for the first time, and say to her: "Although we do not know each other, you are like a sister to me. Do you want to know why? Because I am a Bahá'í, and Bahá'u'lláh, the Manifestation of God for today has told us to love all His creatures. In every human being, I see the face of the Almighty Creator."

4. When we teach the Faith, we should not be excessively liberal. Decide in which of the following situations you are being too liberal. Mark them with an "L".

___L___ Someone who is investigating the Faith asks you if there are any leaders in the Bahá'í community. You respond: "We don't have priests or clergy that come between us and God. We all live according to our own conscience. Nobody tells us what to do."

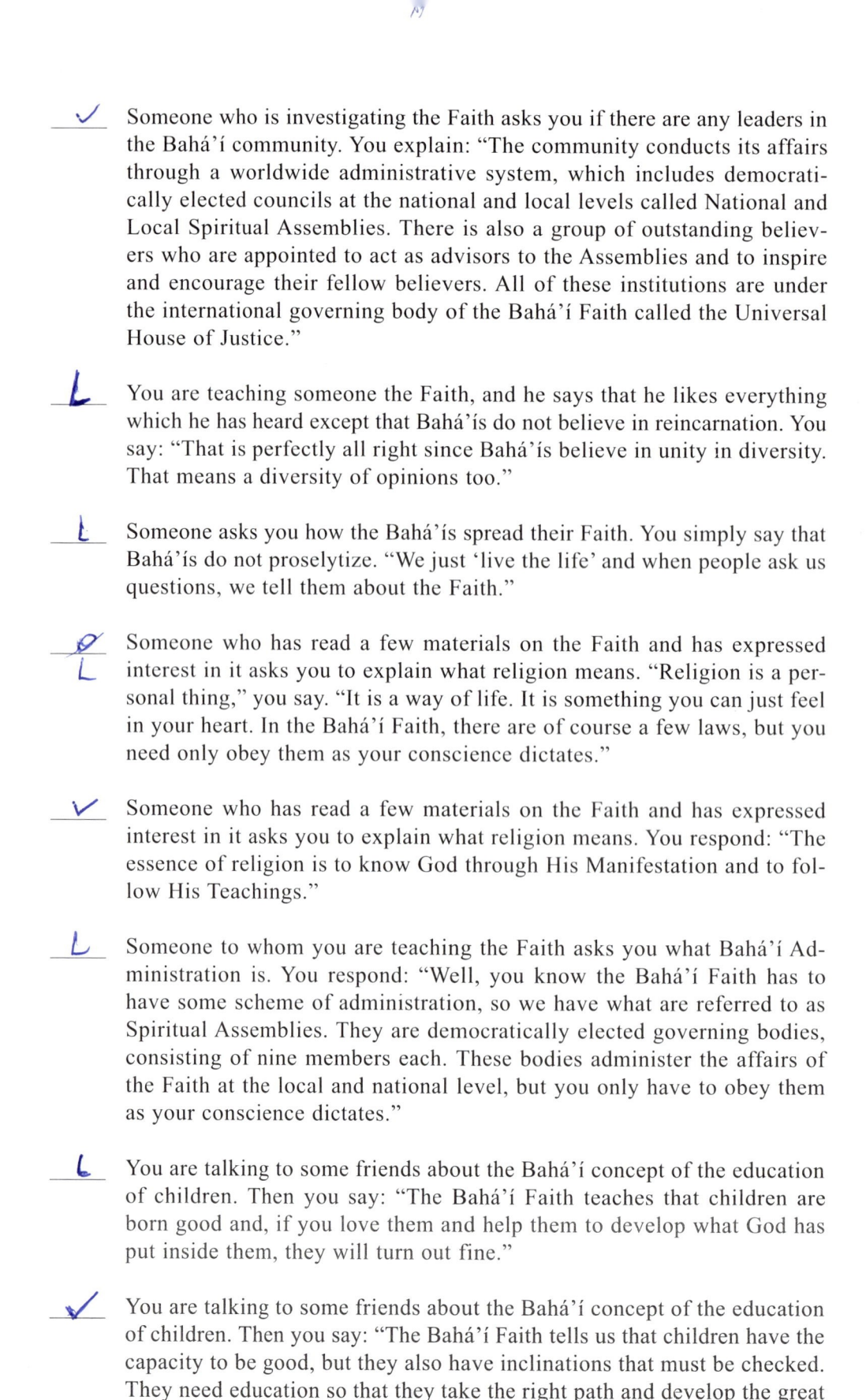

____ ✓ ____ Someone who is investigating the Faith asks you if there are any leaders in the Bahá'í community. You explain: "The community conducts its affairs through a worldwide administrative system, which includes democratically elected councils at the national and local levels called National and Local Spiritual Assemblies. There is also a group of outstanding believers who are appointed to act as advisors to the Assemblies and to inspire and encourage their fellow believers. All of these institutions are under the international governing body of the Bahá'í Faith called the Universal House of Justice."

____ L ____ You are teaching someone the Faith, and he says that he likes everything which he has heard except that Bahá'ís do not believe in reincarnation. You say: "That is perfectly all right since Bahá'ís believe in unity in diversity. That means a diversity of opinions too."

____ L ____ Someone asks you how the Bahá'ís spread their Faith. You simply say that Bahá'ís do not proselytize. "We just 'live the life' and when people ask us questions, we tell them about the Faith."

____ ∅/L ____ Someone who has read a few materials on the Faith and has expressed interest in it asks you to explain what religion means. "Religion is a personal thing," you say. "It is a way of life. It is something you can just feel in your heart. In the Bahá'í Faith, there are of course a few laws, but you need only obey them as your conscience dictates."

____ ✓ ____ Someone who has read a few materials on the Faith and has expressed interest in it asks you to explain what religion means. You respond: "The essence of religion is to know God through His Manifestation and to follow His Teachings."

____ L ____ Someone to whom you are teaching the Faith asks you what Bahá'í Administration is. You respond: "Well, you know the Bahá'í Faith has to have some scheme of administration, so we have what are referred to as Spiritual Assemblies. They are democratically elected governing bodies, consisting of nine members each. These bodies administer the affairs of the Faith at the local and national level, but you only have to obey them as your conscience dictates."

____ L ____ You are talking to some friends about the Bahá'í concept of the education of children. Then you say: "The Bahá'í Faith teaches that children are born good and, if you love them and help them to develop what God has put inside them, they will turn out fine."

____ ✓ ____ You are talking to some friends about the Bahá'í concept of the education of children. Then you say: "The Bahá'í Faith tells us that children have the capacity to be good, but they also have inclinations that must be checked. They need education so that they take the right path and develop the great potential with which they are each endowed.

5. Decide which of the responses would be appropriate in each of the situations below, as you try to determine how to go about teaching the Faith. One or more of the choices may apply to each.

    a. Be wary
    b. Be bold
    c. Act swiftly
    d. Mark time
    e. ✓ Use the direct method
    f. ✓ Use the indirect method
    g. Be challenging
    h. Be conciliatory

__c, e__ Someone comes to the local Bahá'í Center very excited. She says that she has read something about the Faith in a pamphlet and wants to know more about Bahá'u'lláh. She explains that she has always felt deep in her heart that God would never abandon humanity and that He would send us another Manifestation.

__f & d__ You and your family have moved to a village where you do not know anyone. One day, shorty after your arrival, your neighbor comes to your home to welcome you and to introduce himself. In doing so, he makes it clear that all the villagers are very united in their religion and that they do not like the way these "other" religions come and try to divide people.

__b__ You and your family have moved to a village where you do not know anyone. One day, shortly after your arrival, your neighbor comes to your home to welcome you and to introduce himself. He notices the picture of 'Abdu'l-Bahá that you have placed in your new home and asks: "Who is that Man?"

__f, a__ You have joined an organization of people interested in promoting peace. One of the individuals particularly attracted to the ideas you express in the meetings firmly believes that the only way to achieve meaningful change in society is through partisan political action. He makes it a point to talk with you each time the organization meets.

__f__ One of the people with whom you work has told you on several occasions that he does not believe in God. Yet he is attracted to many of the ideas you express related to social issues, for example, the equality of men and women and the need for universal education.

__e, c__ At a village meeting attended by the head of one of the political parties of the region, you put forward some ideas about the education of children. Afterwards, the party head comes over to talk to you. He says that he knows you are a Bahá'í and likes many of the suggestions you made. He is interested in learning more about the Faith.

__a__ One of the newly enrolled believers takes you to her home to meet her family. They are opposed to her being a Bahá'í and are trying to get her to leave the Faith.

The Qualities and Attitudes of the Teacher - 69

_b_ One of the newly enrolled believers takes you to her home to meet her family. She tells you that they are all very excited about the Faith and cannot wait to hear more.

_a,d_ You are living in a country where the government has forbidden the Bahá'ís to organize formally or hold large meetings.

6. Give an example of each of the following:

Being contemptuous of the poor: _____

Being timid before the great: _____

Overstressing the truth: _____

Whittling down the truth: _____

SECTION 17

The following guidance from the Guardian reminds us that, as in all things, we should look to 'Abdu'l-Bahá when we try to determine the most appropriate approach to teaching in any situation:

> "Let us too bear in mind the example which our beloved Master has clearly set before us. Wise and tactful in His approach, wakeful and attentive in His early intercourse, broad and liberal in all His public utterances, cautious and gradual in the unfolding of the essential verities of the Cause, passionate in His appeal yet sober in argument, confident in tone, unswerving in conviction, dignified in His manners—such were the distinguishing features of our Beloved's noble presentation of the Cause of Bahá'u'lláh." [23]

1. As you strive to follow the example of 'Abdu'l-Bahá, what will you be like in your approach to teaching? _____

2. What will you try to be like when you first come into contact with a person? __
   _____

3. What will characterize your public statements? _____

4. How will you bring to the attention of people the truths of the Cause? _____
   _____

5. What will you strive to be like in your appeal? _____

6. In your argument? _____

7. In your tone? _____

8. In your conviction? _____

9. In your manners? _____

Now memorize the above quotation.

SECTION 18

We began this unit by reminding ourselves that "being" and "doing" are complementary and inseparable aspects of a spiritual life. Then we devoted several sections to exploring some of the spiritual qualities that we must all strive to develop as we engage in regular and systematic teaching activity. Our discussion of humility led us to consider our attitude towards learning. Next we discussed a few other important attitudes that a teacher of the Cause must possess. Now let us go one step further and explore the nature of our relationship with those we teach. What should these relationships be like? What do the writings tell us about this?

The first concept that probably comes to mind is fellowship. Clearly, in the context of personal teaching plans, the ability to establish bonds of friendship with people is essential. This same ability, even in certain types of projects, when, for example, we are teaching people we hardly know, is crucial, for it determines how we approach them, how we communicate with them, and how successful we are in touching their hearts.

A question we need to ask ourselves is how we are to develop the ability to establish warm relationships with people. Our temperaments, of course, are different. Some of us, whether as a result of our upbringing or a natural inclination, find it easy to make friends. Some can strike up a conversation with perfect strangers. Others are shy and find this more of a challenge. Yet, no matter what our character, we should realize that, through conscious effort, we can learn to consort with people in a spirit of fellowship. The writings offer numerous and valuable counsels on this subject, only a few examples of which are given below. The phrases set off by quotation marks are taken directly from the writings themselves. It is suggested that you read through the ideas several times and discuss them in your group.

> We are told to tear away the "curtain of foreignness" and to "know all as friends". We are expected to "befriend all nations and communities", not look upon "violence, force, evil intentions, persecutions or hostility", but raise our eyes to "the horizon of glory" and consider each of God's creatures as "a sign of the Lord".

> We are called upon to "associate and sympathize with both friends and strangers", "with infinite kindness and love", and not to look "at all upon the merits and capabilities" of others.

> If a soul is "seeking to quarrel", we should ask for "reconciliation". If he blames us, we should "praise" him. If he gives us a "deadly poison", we should bestow an "all-healing antidote". If he creates "death", we should administer "eternal life". If he becomes a "thorn", we should change into "roses and hyacinths".

> We should endeavor so that "all the nations and communities of the world, even the enemies, put their trust, assurance and hope" in us. If a person "falls into errors a hundred-thousand times", he should be able to "turn his face" to us, "hopeful" that we will forgive him; for he must not become "hopeless, neither grieved nor despondent."

> We must "powerfully sustain one another and seek for everlasting life", and become "the mercies and the blessings sent forth" by God.

> We are told to be "in sympathy" with others. "In great tenderness" should we "blow the breath of life" into them and "call them to God". We should "consider love and union as a delectable paradise, and count annoyance and hostility as the torment of hell-fire."

> We must be careful not to "harm any soul, or make any heart to sorrow". We should not "offend the feelings of another, even though he be an evil-doer". We are urged not to look "upon the creatures", but to turn ourselves to "their Creator".

> We are called upon to "sacrifice" ourselves for the "well-being of the people" and to be a "kind comforter to all the inhabitants of the world." We should weep "at the misfortunes" of God's creatures and become "grieved at the distress" of God's children. We should be "kind to all people and pained at the sight of the calamities of the inhabitants of the world."

> We are called upon to be "loving fathers to the orphan, and a refuge to the helpless, and a treasury for the poor, and a cure for the ailing." We are to be "the helpers of every victim of oppression, the patrons of the disadvantaged." We should think "at all times of rendering some service to every member of the human race."

We should "exert" ourselves to "purify the hearts" as much as we can, and "bestow abundant effort in rejoicing the souls." We should "do some good to every person whose path" we cross and "be of some benefit to him." We must endeavor to "improve the character of each and all, and reorient the minds of men." Ours is the task to "summon" the people to God and "invite" humanity to "follow the example of the Company on high."

If we desire to "soften the hearts" and bring our friends "under the shadow of the Tree of Life", we should show forth "firmness and integrity". Our "sincerity and severance" should "day by day increase" until "by the power of the Truth" shall we "soften and subdue the hearts" and "awaken the souls". We should "show forth such power, such endurance, as to astonish all beholders."

We are called upon to bring "life to the dead, and awaken those who slumber." "In the darkness of the world" we are to be "radiant flames". "In the sands of perdition" we are to be "well-springs of the water of life" and "guidance from the Lord God."

You may now wish to memorize the following quotation from the Writings of 'Abdu'l-Bahá:

"As for you, O ye lovers of God, make firm your steps in His Cause, with such resolve that ye shall not be shaken though the direst of calamities assail the world. By nothing, under no conditions, be ye perturbed. Be ye anchored fast as the high mountains, be stars that dawn over the horizon of life, be bright lamps in the gatherings of unity, be souls humble and lowly in the presence of the friends, be innocent in heart. Be ye symbols of guidance and lights of godliness, severed from the world, clinging to the handhold that is sure and strong, spreading abroad the spirit of life, riding the Ark of salvation. Be ye daysprings of generosity, dawning-points of the mysteries of existence, sites where inspiration alighteth, rising-places of splendors, souls that are sustained by the Holy Spirit, enamored of the Lord, detached from all save Him, holy above the characteristics of humankind, clothed in the attributes of the angels of heaven, that ye may win for yourselves the highest bestowal of all, in this new time, this wondrous age." [24]

SECTION 19

As we consort with all people in a spirit of fellowship, and through our efforts to live a Bahá'í life, we attract others to the Cause. We are not, of course, expected to be perfect, nor do we claim to be free of shortcomings. Yet to the extent that we show forth the qualities of a Bahá'í do we become distinguished and influence those around us. It is in this sense that we often talk about teaching by example. But we should be careful that the phrase "teaching by example" does not become an excuse for not teaching. It is true that we need to pay a great deal of attention to our inner condition, to our character, to our deeds, and to the rectitude of our conduct. But this should not make us lose sight of the fact that it is with the key of our utterance that we are to open the gates to the city of the human heart. To clarify this point, let us look at two sets of quotations from the writings and try to understand them together. First read the following quotations:

> "Whoso ariseth among you to teach the Cause of his Lord, let him, before all else, teach his own self, that his speech may attract the hearts of them that hear him. Unless he teacheth his own self, the words of his mouth will not influence the heart of the seeker." [25]

> "One thing and only one thing will unfailingly and alone secure the undoubted triumph of this sacred Cause, namely the extent to which our own inner life and private character mirror forth in their manifold aspects the splendor of those eternal principles proclaimed by Bahá'u'lláh." [26]

> "Whoso ariseth, in this Day, to aid Our Cause, and summoneth to his assistance the hosts of a praiseworthy character and upright conduct, the influence flowing from such an action will, most certainly, be diffused throughout the whole world." [27]

> "Let your actions cry aloud to the world that you are indeed Bahá'ís, for it is actions that speak to the world and are the cause of the progress of humanity.

> "If we are true Bahá'ís speech is not needed. Our actions will help on the world, will spread civilization, will help the progress of science, and cause the arts to develop. Without action nothing in the material world can be accomplished, neither can words unaided advance a man in the spiritual Kingdom. It is not through lip-service only that the elect of God have attained to holiness, but by patient lives of active service they have brought light into the world." [28]

Now study the following set of quotations:

> "It is at such times that the friends of God avail themselves of the occasion, seize the opportunity, rush forth and win the prize. If their task is to be confined to good conduct and advice, nothing will be accomplished. They must speak out, expound the proofs, set forth clear arguments, draw irrefutable conclusions establishing the truth of the manifestation of the Sun of Reality." [29]

> "Then look thou not at the degree of thy capacity, look thou at the boundless favor of Bahá'u'lláh; all-encompassing is His bounty, and consummate His grace." [30]

> "Turn thy face toward the Kingdom of God, ask for the bestowals of the Holy Spirit, speak, and the confirmations of the Spirit will come." [31]

> "O ye beloved of God! Repose not yourselves on your couches, nay bestir yourselves as soon as ye recognize your Lord, the Creator, and hear of the things which have befallen Him, and hasten to His assistance. Unloose your tongues, and proclaim unceasingly His Cause. This shall be better for you than all the treasures of the past and of the future, if ye be of them that comprehend this truth." [32]

> "If the friends always waited until they were fully qualified to do any particular task, the work of the Cause would be almost at a standstill! But the very act of striving to serve, however unworthy one may feel, attracts the blessings of God and enables one to become more fitted for the task.
>
> "Today the need is so great on the part of humanity to hear of the Divine Message, that the believers must plunge into the work, wherever and however they can, heedless of their own shortcomings, but ever heedful of the crying need of their fellow-men to hear of the Teachings in their darkest hour of travail." [33]

If we separate the first set of quotations from all the other passages on the subject of teaching—only a few examples of which are given in the second set—and focus solely on them, we may end up using them as an excuse for not teaching. We fall into this trap when we mistakenly arrive at the conclusion that our main task is to improve our own inner condition and become better and better people until we reach the point where we are so perfect that we do not need words to teach, because others will be attracted to us and will go out of their way to investigate the Faith by themselves. Yet we know that 'Abdu'l-Bahá, who led a life of deeds more exemplary than any of ours, used the power of His utterance and, at every appropriate opportunity, spoke about the Faith.

What is important to realize is that the main theme of the first set of quotations is not how to teach the Faith. These passages reveal to us profound spiritual truths about the influence flowing from our inner condition and about the power of good deeds and upright conduct. They remind us that our actions cannot contradict our words. If one is going to teach honesty, for example, one should sincerely strive to be honest.

In general, it is not wise to take a vast, profound subject, such as teaching, and draw conclusions about it on the basis of one or two quotations.

With these thoughts in mind, let us go back and think about the above passages. Fill in the blanks with the appropriate words:

1. Whoever arises to teach the Cause of his Lord, let him, before all else, *teach his ownself*.

2. Unless one teaches one's own self, *the words of his mouth will not influence the hearts of seeker*.

3. One thing and only one thing will unfailingly and alone secure the undoubted triumph of the Cause, namely, *the extent to which our own inner life and private character mirror forth the manifold aspects the splendor of those eternal principles proclaimed by baha'u'llah*.

4. Whoever arises, in this Day, to aid the Cause of God, and summons to his assistance _the host of a praiseworthy character and upright conduct_, the influence flowing from such an action will, most certainly, _will be defused throughout the whole world_.

5. It is actions that _speaks to the world_ and are the cause of _progress of the world_.

6. If we are true Bahá'ís, _speech is not needed_. Our actions should cry aloud to the world that _man are indeed bahai_.

7. Our actions should _help all the world_, should _help the progress of science_, should _cause the arts to develop_, and _____.

8. Without action, _nothing in the material world can be accomplished_, neither can words _unaided advance a man in the spiritual kingdom_.

9. It is not through lip-service that those near to God have attained to holiness, but by _patience lives of active service they have brought light into the world_.

10. If our task is to be confined to good conduct and advice, _nothing will be accomplished_. We must _speak_ out, _expound_ the proofs, _set forth_ clear arguments, _draw irrefutable conclusions_ establishing the truth of the manifestation of the Sun of Reality.

11. We should not look at the degree of our capacity, but at the _boundless favor_.

12. We should turn our faces towards the Kingdom of God, _ask for the bestowal of holy spirits_, speak, and _true confirmation of the holy spirit will come_.

13. We should not repose on our couches, but should _bestir yourselves_ as soon as we recognize our Lord, the Creator, and hear of the things which have befallen Him, _hasten to his assistance_.

76 - The Qualities and Attitudes of the Teacher

14. We are to unloose our tongues and _proclaim unceasingly his cause_. This is better for us than _all the treasures of the past and the future_.

15. If we always waited until we were fully qualified to do any particular task, _the work of the cause will be almost at standstill_.

16. The very act of striving to serve, however unworthy we may feel, _attracts the blessings of God and enables one to become more fitted for the task_.

17. Today the need is so great on the part of humanity to hear of the Divine Message, that we must _plunge into the work_, whatever and however we can, _heedless of our own shortcomings_, but ever heedful of _the crying need of the fellowmen to hear of the teachings_ in their darkest hour of travail.

SECTION 20

Let us end this unit on the qualities and attitudes of the teacher with one more thought. We have already said in the previous unit that, when teaching a person the Faith, we are not talking to some abstract entity called "humanity". Nor are people just empty containers waiting to be filled up with information. They have their own hopes and aspirations, their own fears and difficulties. As teachers of the Cause, it is their souls to which we must speak, souls that have been created to know God and to love Him. We should address ourselves to both their hearts and their minds in order to ignite the spark of faith and assist them in reaching the shores of true understanding. In this context, the following accounts left by one of the early believers in the West, describing how 'Abdu'l-Bahá offered His Father's Message to those He encountered, will prepare us for the next unit in which we will explore the act of teaching itself:

> "And when, under His encouraging sympathy, the interviewer became emptied of his words, there followed a brief interval of silence. There was no instant and complete outpouring of explanation and advice. He sometimes closed His eyes a moment as if He sought guidance from above Himself; sometimes sat and searched the questioner's soul with a loving, comprehending smile that melted the heart."[34]

> "And He never argued, of course. Nor did He press a point. He left one free. There was never an assumption of authority, rather He was ever the personification of humility. He taught 'as if offering a gift to a king.' He never told me what I should do, beyond suggesting that what I was doing was right. Nor did He ever tell me what I should believe. He made Truth and Love so beautiful and royal that the

heart perforce did reverence. He showed me by His voice, manner, bearing, smile, how I should be, knowing that out of the pure soil of being the good fruit of deeds and words would surely spring.

"There was a strange, awe-inspiring mingling of humility and majesty, relaxation and power in His slightest word or gesture which made me long to understand its source. What made Him so different, so immeasurably superior to any other man I had ever met?" [35]

"I have mentioned several times the impression He always made upon me of an all-embracing love. How rarely we receive such an impression from those around us, even from our nearest and dearest, we all know. All our human love seems based upon self, and even its highest expression is limited to one or to a very few. Not so was the love which radiated from 'Abdu'l-Bahá. Like the sun it poured upon all alike and, like it, also warmed and gave new life to all it touch." [36]

"No matter what subject was brought up He was perfectly at home in its discussion, yet always with an undercurrent of modesty and loving consideration for the opinions of others. I have before spoken of His unfailing courtesy. It was really more than what that term usually connotes to the Western mind. The same Persian word is used for both reverence and courtesy. He 'saw the Face of His Heavenly Father in every face' and reverenced the soul behind it. How could one be discourteous if such an attitude was held towards everyone!" [37]

"In all of my many opportunities of meeting, of listening to and talking with 'Abdu'l-Bahá I was impressed, and constantly more deeply impressed, with His method of teaching souls. That is the word. He did not attempt to reach the mind alone. He sought the soul, the reality of every one He met. Oh, He could be logical, even scientific in His presentation of an argument, as He demonstrated constantly in the many addresses I have heard Him give and the many more I have read. But it was not the logic of the schoolman, not the science of the classroom. His slightest word, His slightest association with a soul was shot through with an illuminating radiance which lifted the hearer to a higher plane of consciousness. Our hearts burned within us when He spoke." [38]

After reading through the above passages one more time, write a number of sentences describing the attitudes that characterized 'Abdu'l-Bahá's interactions with people and the way He approached His conversations about the Faith, for example: "There was a mingling of humility and majesty in His every word."

1. _____
2. _____
3. _____
4. _____
5. _____
6. _____
7. _____

78 - The Qualities and Attitudes of the Teacher

8. _____
9. _____
10. _____

REFERENCES

1. *Tablets of the Divine Plan* (Wilmette: Bahá'í Publishing Trust, 1993), p. 54.

2. Ibid., p. 72.

3. From a letter dated 8 November 1956 written on behalf of Shoghi Effendi to an individual believer, published in *Teaching the Bahá'í Faith: Compilations and a Statement Prepared by the Research Department of the Universal House of Justice* (Mona Vale: Bahá'í Publications Australia, 1995), no. 156, pp. 84-85.

4. From a letter dated 6 November 1949 written on behalf of Shoghi Effendi to an individual believer, published in *Teaching the Bahá'í Faith*, no. 124, p. 76.

5. *Paris Talks: Addresses given by 'Abdu'l-Bahá in Paris in 1911-1912* (London: Bahá'í Publishing Trust, 1995), p. 64.

6. From a letter dated 1 September 1933 written on behalf of Shoghi Effendi to an individual believer, published in *Teaching the Bahá'í Faith*, no. 92, p. 69.

7. *Selections from the Writings of 'Abdu'l-Bahá* (Wilmette: Bahá'í Publishing Trust, 1997), no. 216, p. 282.

8. From a letter dated 30 June 1937 written on behalf of Shoghi Effendi to an individual believer, published in *Teaching the Bahá'í Faith,* no. 100, p. 71.

9. *Selections from the Writings of 'Abdu'l-Bahá*, no. 213, p. 281.

10. Ibid., no. 214, pp. 281-82.

11. *Gleanings from the Writings of Bahá'u'lláh* (Wilmette: Bahá'í Publishing Trust, 1983), V, p. 8.

12. Ibid., CXXXII, p. 289.

13. Ibid., C, p. 201.

14. *Selections from the Writings of 'Abdu'l-Bahá*, no. 204, p. 263.

15. *Gleanings from the Writings of Bahá'u'lláh*, CXLII, p. 310.

16. Shoghi Effendi, *Bahá'í Administration: Selected Messages 1922-1932* (Wilmette: Bahá'í Publishing Trust, 1974), p. 69.

17. *Selections from the Writings of 'Abdu'l-Bahá*, no. 217, p. 282.

18. Ibid., no. 15, pp. 33-34.

19. From a letter dated 31 March 1932 written on behalf of Shoghi Effendi to an individual believer, published in *Teaching the Bahá'í Faith*, no. 91, pp. 68-69.

20. The Universal House of Justice, *Wellspring of Guidance: Messages 1963-1968* (Wilmette: Bahá'í Publishing Trust, 1976), p. 33.

21. From the 1974 Naw-Rúz message written by the Universal House of Justice to the Bahá'ís of the world, published in *Promoting Entry by Troops* (Riviera Beach: Palabra Publications, 1996), no. 32, p. 33.

22. Shoghi Effendi, *Citadel of Faith: Messages to America 1947-1957* (Wilmette: Bahá'í Publishing Trust, 1965), pp. 25-26.

23. *Bahá'í Administration: Selected Messages 1922-1932*, pp. 69-70.

24. *Selections from the Writings of 'Abdu'l-Bahá*, no. 199, p. 253.

25. *Gleanings from the Writings of Bahá'u'lláh*, CXXVIII, p. 277.

26. *Bahá'í Administration: Selected Messages 1922-1932*, p. 66.

27. *Gleanings from the Writings of Bahá'u'lláh*, CXXXI, p. 287.

28. *Paris Talks: Addresses given by 'Abdu'l-Bahá in Paris in 1911-1912*, pp. 77-78.

29. *Selections from the Writings of 'Abdu'l-Bahá*, no. 212, p. 280.

30. Ibid., no. 153, p. 188.

31. Ibid., no. 153, p. 188.

32. *Gleanings from the Writings of Bahá'u'lláh*, CLIV, p. 330.

33. From a letter dated 4 May 1942 written on behalf of Shoghi Effendi to an individual believer, published in *Teaching the Bahá'í Faith*, no. 104, p. 72.

34. Howard Colby Ives, *Portals to Freedom* (Oxford: George Ronald, 1983), p. 195.

35. Ibid., pp. 39-40.

36. Ibid., p. 45.

37. Ibid., p. 116.

38. Ibid., p. 39.

The Act of Teaching

Purpose

To become familiar with some of the approaches
and methods of personal teaching endeavors
and collective campaigns.

Practice

To design and implement your own personal teaching plan
and to participate in at least one teaching campaign.

SECTION 1

Having explored the spiritual nature of teaching in the first unit, and the qualities and attitudes of the teacher in the second, we now turn our attention to the act of teaching itself. In doing so we should be careful not to define teaching as the mere proclamation of the Faith. Proclamation is a highly meritorious and necessary activity to be carried out both by individuals and by communities. Yet, the opening of the gates of the city of a human heart to Bahá'u'lláh is not, in general, accomplished through an act of proclamation, no matter how elaborate its design or how professional its execution. Teaching includes proclamation, but its main purpose is to help others recognize Bahá'u'lláh as the Manifestation of God for today, to deepen them and to assist them in becoming confirmed in their newly acquired Faith. The Universal House of Justice explains this all-important distinction in these words:

> **"The proclamation of the Faith, following established plans and aiming to use on an increasing scale the facilities of mass communication must be vigorously pursued. It should be remembered that the purpose of proclamation is to make known to all mankind the fact and general aim of the new Revelation, while teaching programs should be planned to confirm individuals from every stratum of society."** [1]

It is clear from the above passage that proclamation activities should be organized so as to familiarize people with the noble aims and ideals of the Cause and help develop in them a positive attitude towards the Faith. It is possible, of course, that in this process, a highly receptive soul becomes enamored with the Faith and, after some investigation, decides to enroll in it. However, we should not expect, at least at this stage in human history, that proclamation alone will lead to a significant increase in the number of believers. The purpose of teaching is not achieved by giving information out to people and leaving them to themselves. Teaching involves dialogue, conversations between confirmed believers and those who are willing to listen and investigate the truth of Bahá'u'lláh's Revelation. To explore this point further, carry out the following exercise:

1. One of the best ways to teach the Faith is through firesides. Firesides are warm and intimate meetings held in one's home to which those interested in the Faith are invited. They provide excellent opportunities for the exchange of ideas and fruitful conversation which can lead people to the acceptance of Bahá'u'lláh. However, if care is not taken, a fireside can easily turn into a proclamation event.

    a. Suppose you are holding a weekly fireside in your home. You begin each meeting by welcoming your guests and asking one of the Bahá'ís present to recite a prayer. Then the invited speaker gives a talk for about thirty to forty-five minutes on a particular subject, for example, Bahá'í education, Bahá'í family life, the oneness of humankind or the unity of religion. At the end, you ask for questions, and usually there are only one or two. Refreshments are then served, and your guests depart. Would you agree that a meeting of this kind, which in itself is highly meritorious, has more the characteristics of proclamation? _____

b. Suppose that after a while, you decide to change the character of the meetings. So, for each fireside, you invite one or two talented friends to give a short musical performance after the talk, rightfully hoping that the introduction of music will heighten the spiritual atmosphere of the event. Do you think that by doing this you have changed the fireside from a proclamation to a teaching event? _____

c. What are some of the ways through which you could make the fireside more of a teaching activity? _____

_____
_____
_____
_____
_____
_____
_____
_____

SECTION 2

One of the purposes of proclamation is to find receptive souls with whom we can share the Message of Bahá'u'lláh more intimately. The ability to recognize receptive individuals is crucial to success in teaching, both as we pursue our own personal teaching plans and when we participate in the projects devised by our institutions. Of course, as teachers of the Cause, we need to pray continually that God may lead us to those whose hearts He has prepared to receive His Message. But then, we must be able to recognize them when we meet them. This is not always easy. Even in the case of a teaching campaign carried out among a highly receptive population, not everyone will want to hear the Message and embrace its truth; it is left to the teacher to find those souls ready to respond to Bahá'u'lláh's call.

A receptive person may not necessarily appear to be searching for the Faith, or even be particularly interested in religion. In fact, it is important to realize that receptivity and spirituality are not the same. What is required is a condition in which a person is willing to listen to the Teachings and explore their truth with a degree of openness. As we gain experience in teaching, and as our spiritual faculties become sharper and sharper, our ability to sense this condition increases.

Although it is impossible to lay down hard and fast rules about what makes a person receptive, we can identify some of the contributing factors. These often make people more receptive at certain points in their lives for a particular length of time. This is true of both individuals and whole populations. Discuss this subject in your group and write down some of the factors that you think can affect a person's receptivity, such as the following example:

1. <u>Becoming aware of widespread injustice in the world.</u>
2. _____
3. _____
4. _____
5. _____
6. _____
7. _____
8. _____
9. _____
10. _____

It is suggested that, before moving on to the next section, you memorize the following passage written by Shoghi Effendi. It speaks of the relation between the present-day turmoil in the world and people's receptivity to the Cause. Some of the words are difficult, so it would be helpful for you to discuss the meaning of the passage in your group. As you commit it to memory, think about the implications of the Guardian's statement for your teaching efforts.

> **"The opportunities which the turmoil of the present age presents, with all the sorrows which it evokes, the fears which it excites, the disillusionment which it produces, the perplexities which it creates, the indignation which it arouses, the revolt which it provokes, the grievances it engenders, the spirit of restless search which it awakens, must, in like manner, be exploited for the purpose of spreading far and wide, the knowledge of the redemptive power of the Faith of Bahá'u'lláh, and for enlisting fresh recruits in the ever-swelling army of His followers. So precious an opportunity, so rare a conjunction of favorable circumstances, may never again recur."** [2]

SECTION 3

When we find people who are receptive, we enter into a conversation with them, sometimes relatively brief and sometimes ongoing, the purpose of which is to help them recognize Bahá'u'lláh's Station. But what should the substance of these conversations be? What should we say to those we teach?

You already know, of course, that the answer to this question is by no means simple. There is no formula that we can learn and repeat to everyone in every situation. The individuals with whom we have such intimate conversations are each in a particular spiritual state with varied needs and questions. As teachers of the Cause, we must reflect constantly on how the verities of the Faith are to be explained to every seeker—what is to be said, and in what sequence should thoughts be expressed.

Yet, while we should be aware of individual differences, we should not make the mistake of overemphasizing them to the point that we lose sight of the underlying unity of human existence. The way people respond to the Message of Bahá'u'lláh follows certain patterns, and these patterns become especially noticeable among those of the same culture and background. If you are a student, for example, and you set out to teach among your peers, you will gradually find one introductory explanation that proves to be effective with most of your friends. The details of this presentation will change as, on each occasion, different questions are asked and different interests are expressed. But the basic pattern will remain the same.

As you begin to think systematically about the way you will explain the Faith to others, you may find it useful to consider two aspects of the message you will convey. The first is information. The listener will, naturally, want to know a number of facts about the Faith. When did it begin? How large is the Bahá'í community? How widespread is it? Do Bahá'ís believe in an afterlife? What are the basic principles of the Bahá'í Faith? As you can imagine, the number of facts related to the Faith is overwhelmingly large. What information you will offer to a person on a given occasion will depend on the nature of your conversation. But there are some things a seeker usually needs to learn during his or her initial stages of investigation, and it is quite instructive to think about these. In the space below, write down some of the information that you think would be helpful. You should not be too critical in making your list. You will be asked to review and modify it after we have discussed a few other points in the subsequent sections.

The Bab - Bahaullah's life and attributes, Funda Principles of the faith - Spirituality and Unity

How bahai people serve humanity and strive for the betterment of the world

Progressive revelation - time for religion

88 - The Act of Teaching

_____
_____
_____
_____
_____
_____
_____
_____
_____
_____

Now compare your list with those of your friends.

SECTION 4

In the previous section, we examined one aspect of the message we convey to people in our efforts to teach the Faith, namely, information. But is teaching the same as giving out information? Consider, for example, the fact, most central to Bahá'í belief, that Bahá'u'lláh is the Manifestation of God for today. The statement "Bahá'ís believe that Bahá'u'lláh is the Manifestation of God for today" by itself is only an item of information, admittedly the most important item of information in the universe. Yet, is the mere pronouncement of this fact sufficient to help most people recognize the Station of Bahá'u'lláh?

Now consider something which, though related to this fact, is not simply information, namely, the concept that "Bahá'u'lláh is the Manifestation of God for today". While a piece of information needs only to be given and received, absorbing a concept involves understanding. What does Bahá'u'lláh mean by "God" and by "Manifestation", and what is the nature of His claim to be the Manifestation of God for today?

Another example is the statement "Bahá'ís obey the laws brought by Bahá'u'lláh." As it stands, this statement is clearly an item of information, again a very important one. But simply providing this information is a very small part of explaining to someone that, as a Bahá'í, he or she will have to obey certain laws. For that to be done, it is necessary to help the person gain at least some understanding of several related ideas, for example, the profoundly beautiful concept of "law" as described by Bahá'u'lláh when He calls His laws **"the lamps of My loving providence among My servants, and the keys of My mercy for My creatures."** [3]

Once you have made a distinction between information and concepts, you will have no difficulty identifying a significant number of concepts, the understanding of which will help seekers recognize Bahá'u'lláh and join the ranks of His followers. Try to make such a list. Again write down all the concepts that come to your mind, without worrying about the length of your list or its order. You will come back and review it later.

_____
_____

The Act of Teaching - 89

Now compare your list with those of your friends.

SECTION 5

Having considered these ideas, let us now focus our discussion on the initial presentation you will give when explaining the Faith to someone who knows little about it. Remember that your aim is to help open the gates of the city of the seeker's heart to Bahá'u'lláh. Through your presentation, you will provide the listener with certain information and assist him or her in understanding several fundamental concepts. Clearly, the central concept you want to get across is that Bahá'u'lláh is the Manifestation of God for today. For it is on the basis of this understanding that he or she will decide to join the Bahá'í community. Keeping this central concept in mind, then, you will have to say a number of things, all of which will help to make the concept clear and lead the seeker to the recognition of the Station of Bahá'u'lláh.

In choosing the concepts and the information you will present, and the order in which you will do so, you will need to pay close attention to the passage written by the Universal House of Justice indicating at what point a seeker is to be considered a Bahá'í:

> **"Those who declare themselves as Bahá'ís should become enchanted with the beauty of the Teachings, and touched by the love of Bahá'u'lláh. The declarants need not know all the proofs, history, laws, and principles of the Faith, but in the process of declaring themselves they must, in addition to catching the spark of faith, become basically informed about the Central Figures of the Faith, as well as the existence of laws they must follow and an administration they must obey."** [4]

Now, go back to the lists of concepts and information you prepared in the previous sections. On the basis of the above words of the Universal House of Justice, decide what you would add to your list of information and what you would discard. Make a new list, placing the items in the order you would present them in an introduction to the Faith. Do the same with your list of concepts.

Information:

The Act of Teaching - 91

Concepts:

SECTION 6

To help you to think further about the concepts and information you will present when explaining the Faith to someone for the first time, we will take an imaginary situation and analyze what is being said.

Anna is a seventeen-year-old youth who lives with her family in a small village and attends school in a nearby town. She was raised a Catholic and became a Bahá'í five years ago, after learning about the Faith from her older brother. Since then, she has been active in the Bahá'í community, participating in regional and national teaching campaigns and attending institute courses regularly. With the help of another youth in her village, she also gives a Bahá'í children's class once a week.

Emilia attends the same school as Anna. She was also raised a Catholic. She has heard of the Bahá'í Faith before, but knows very little about it. She has been curious for some time to find out what it means for her friend, Anna, to be a Bahá'í. As to her own beliefs, she has not been concerned much about religion, but she carries the love of Christ in her heart and is a good person.

Since Anna and Emilia became friends, they have often talked about the condition of the world and their hopes for the future. From the comments Emilia has made, Anna realizes that she is receptive to the Faith.

In the sections that follow, you will read Anna's introductory remarks as she begins to teach her friend. You should study them well and carry out the corresponding exercises with great care. These exercises are designed to help you reach some conclusions about how you will explain the Faith to different groups of people. Before moving on to these sections, mention some of the groups of people you are most likely to teach.

SECTION 7

Here is how Anna begins her explanation of the Faith to Emilia:

> From our previous conversations, you know that the Bahá'í Faith is a world religion whose purpose is to unite all the races and peoples in one universal Cause and one common Faith. Bahá'ís are the followers of Bahá'u'lláh, Who they believe is the Promised One of all Ages. As you know, the traditions of almost every people include the promise of a future when peace and harmony will be established on earth and humankind will live in prosperity. We believe that the promised hour has come and that Bahá'u'lláh is the great Personage Whose Teachings will enable humanity to build a new world. In one of His Writings, Bahá'u'lláh says:
>
> **"That which the Lord hath ordained as the sovereign remedy and mightiest instrument for the healing of all the world is the union of all its peoples in one universal Cause, one common Faith."** [5]
>
> If it is all right with you, the first of Bahá'u'lláh's Teachings I will describe for you is about God and our relationship with Him. Bahá'u'lláh teaches us that God is unknowable in His Essence. This means that we should not make images of God in our mind, thinking of Him, for example, as a man. In general, that which has been created cannot understand its creator. For instance, a table cannot understand the nature of the carpenter who made it. The carpenter's existence is totally incomprehensible to the objects he makes.
>
> God is the Creator of all things. He has made the heavens and earth, with its mountains and valleys, its deserts and seas, its rivers, its meadows and trees. God has created the animals and God has created the human being. The reason behind our creation, we are told by Bahá'u'lláh, is love. He says:
>
> **"O Son of Man! I loved thy creation, hence I created thee. Wherefore, do thou love Me, that I may name thy name and fill thy soul with the spirit of life."** [6]
>
> So although God's existence is far beyond our understanding, His love touches our lives and our beings ceaselessly. The way this love flows to us is through His Eternal Covenant. According to this Eternal Covenant, God never leaves us alone and without guidance. Whenever humanity moves away from Him and forgets His Teachings, a Manifestation of God appears and makes His Will and Purpose known to us.
>
> The word "manifest" means to reveal, to bring forth something that was not known before. The Manifestations of God are those special Beings Who reveal to humanity the Word and the Will of God; thus when we listen to Them, we are responding to the Call of God.
>
> There is an example from the physical world that helps us to understand the concept of "Manifestation" as taught by Bahá'u'lláh. In this world, the sun is the source of all warmth and light, without which life would not exist on the planet. Yet the sun itself does not descend to earth, and if we tried to approach it, we would be totally consumed.

But suppose we take a well-polished mirror and point it towards the sun. In it we will see the image of the sun, and the more perfectly polished the mirror, the more perfect the image will be. The Manifestations of God are like perfect Mirrors that reflect the Light of God in all its Splendor. And all these Mirrors reflect the same Light. While God is beyond our reach, these perfect Beings come to us from time to time, live among us, give us guidance, and fill us with the energy we need to progress, materially and spiritually.

You are fortunate to have been raised according to the Teachings sent by God to humanity some two thousand years ago through His Manifestation, Christ, Whose Station is that of the Son of God. Now you can receive the Teachings of a new Manifestation, Bahá'u'lláh, Whose title means the Glory of God. Bahá'u'lláh's Teachings, then, are in perfect harmony with the Teachings of Christ, but they address the condition of humanity today. If you think for a moment about the plight of humanity, I am sure you will agree that the time is right for another Manifestation of God to have appeared. Let me recite for you a passage from the Writings of Bahá'u'lláh that speaks about the Day in which we live:

> **"This is the Day in which God's most excellent favors have been poured out upon men, the Day in which His most mighty grace hath been infused into all created things. It is incumbent upon all the peoples of the world to reconcile their differences, and, with perfect unity and peace, abide beneath the shadow of the Tree of His care and loving-kindness."** [7]

Before going on, perhaps I should stop here so that we can discuss any questions you have. What do you think about what I have said up to now?

SECTION 8

Now let us examine what Anna has said thus far. Five aspects of her presentation are analyzed in the exercises below. Mark the statements with which you agree. These exercises do not need lengthy discussion. You should read each statement, examine it, and decide whether or not you agree with it. What is important to remember is that teaching should be approached with an attitude of learning.

1. Anna begins by stating that the Bahá'í Faith is a world religion whose purpose is to unite all peoples and races. She then immediately introduces Bahá'u'lláh as the Promised One of all Ages.

    _____ Immediately introducing Bahá'u'lláh as the Promised One is an excellent way of presenting the Faith to people of all religions—Christians, Muslims, Hindus, Buddhists and others—since the concept of a Promised One exists in every religious tradition in some form or another.

    _____ Most people today are not really interested in religion, even if they belong to one, so it is best not to introduce the Figure of Bahá'u'lláh immediately. It is more effective to talk first about Bahá'í beliefs, explaining in some detail various principles such as the equality of men and women, universal education, and universal peace.

The Act of Teaching - 95

_____ If you are teaching someone who has difficulty believing in God, you could still introduce the Figure of Bahá'u'lláh immediately in your presentation. In that case, however, you would initially refer to Him as One of those Universal Educators Who come to humanity from time to time. Later, you would introduce the concept of "Manifestation of God".

_____ Anna's presentation would be more effective if, having introduced Bahá'u'lláh as the Promised One of all Ages, she went on to cite a number of prophecies to prove to Emilia that He is the fulfillment of each one.

_____ In the vast majority of cases, using prophecies to convince people of the validity of Bahá'u'lláh's Station leads to difficulty. It tends to make people argumentative, rather than putting them in a mood of thoughtful reflection. Anna conveys the important idea that Bahá'u'lláh is the Promised One of all Ages, but is justified in not going into details.

2. After briefly introducing Bahá'u'lláh, Anna speaks about God and man's relationship with Him. Particularly noteworthy is the way she presents these ideas. She does not start by saying "Bahá'ís believe . . .", or much less "I believe . . .". She makes it clear that she is describing the Teachings of Bahá'u'lláh so that the focus of her presentation remains on Him.

_____ In today's world, to talk about God and humanity's relationship with Him too early in our presentation of the Faith will turn people off. Most people are more interested in social issues than in spiritual ones. It would be better for Anna not to bring up the subject.

_____ To explain Bahá'u'lláh's Teaching of God as an Unknowable Essence is highly beneficial for seekers from every religious background and even for those who have difficulty believing in God. It immediately sets the Faith apart from all kinds of superstition and illogical belief. At the same time, it addresses the longing of the seeker's soul to recognize the Source of its being.

3. Anna is careful throughout her presentation to use the word "Manifestation" when referring to Bahá'u'lláh and Christ. The image of the mirror helps her to explain this concept to Emilia.

_____ The word "Manifestation" is too difficult. Anna should use the word "Prophet" since it is both simpler and easier to understand.

_____ A person from a Catholic background would consider it disrespectful to refer to Christ as a Prophet. By the same token, if Anna were to refer to Bahá'u'lláh as a "Prophet", she would give Emilia the impression that His station is beneath that of Christ.

_____ If one is teaching a Muslim, the word "Messenger" could be used effectively, since Muslims refer to Muḥammad as the Messenger of God.

_____ It is correct for Anna to avoid stating explicitly that Bahá'u'lláh is the Return of Christ since the idea of "return" is so confused in the minds of people that there is no way to know what it would mean for Emilia. By using the analogy of the mirror, Anna conveys the concept without confusing the issue.

_____ It is wise for Anna not to dwell on the concept of "Christ as the Son of God". She simply mentions it in passing and then states that Bahá'u'lláh is the Glory of God. By doing so, Anna accepts a certain truth without taking the presentation off its course.

_____ If you were teaching a person from a Hindu background, you would still use the image of the mirror to describe the concept of "Manifestation". But instead of referring to Christ, you would make mention of Lord Krishna's statement: "Whenever there is a decline in righteousness, O Bharat, and the rise of irreligion, it is then that I send forth My spirit. For the salvation of the good, the destruction of the evil-doers, and for firmly establishing righteousness, I manifest myself from age to age."[8]

4. In her presentation, Anna quotes directly from Bahá'u'lláh's Writings a few times.

_____ The words in the quotations are too difficult. It would be better for Anna to avoid quoting directly from the Writings, especially so early in her presentation, and to give the ideas in her own words. Besides, she runs the risk of sounding like a preacher.

_____ Anna weaves the quotations into her presentation in a natural way, very much in keeping with Bahá'u'lláh's own counsel. Even if her friend Emilia does not understand the quotations fully, the words will have an effect on her heart.

5. Anna also uses two analogies to explain difficult concepts. As mentioned above, the analogy of "the sun and the mirror" helps Anna to explain the phrase "Manifestation of God". The other analogy she uses is of the "carpenter and the table" to illustrate the concept that God is beyond human understanding.

_____ If you use analogies when explaining the Faith to people, they think that you are talking down to them. People don't want to be treated like children.

_____ Using analogies is an effective way to teach all people—young or old, illiterate or formally educated. In fact, without analogies, it would be very difficult to understand some of the very profound and abstract ideas contained in the Teachings of the Faith.

SECTION 9

Although Anna stops her presentation to give her friend a chance to express her feelings and ask questions, at this early stage of the conversation, Emilia says little. She merely tells Anna that she likes what she has heard so far, especially the logical way the Bahá'í Faith explain things; it is not at all like the sects that go around and confuse people. Anna then decides to continue her presentation:

> The next of Bahá'u'lláh's Teachings that I would like to present to you is related to the aim of the Bahá'í Faith, which is to unify humanity. In the Bahá'í Teachings we are told that we are the fruits of one tree and the leaves of one branch. Although we differ from one another physically and emotionally, although we have different talents and capacities, we all spring from the same root; we all belong to the same human family.
>
> Humanity can be likened to a vast garden in which grow side by side flowers of every form, color and perfume. The charm and beauty of the garden lie in this diversity. We should not allow the differences that exist among us—in our physical characteristics, our temperaments, our backgrounds, our thoughts and opinions—to give rise to conflict and strife. We should see the members of the human race as beautiful flowers growing in the garden of humanity and rejoice in belonging to this garden.
>
> Although the oneness of humankind is an undeniable truth, the peoples of earth are so far from it that unifying them is no easy task. If you choose to join the Bahá'í community—and it would bring me so much happiness if you would do so—you will participate with the rest of us in our efforts to build and maintain unity. We are all striving to bring our thoughts and actions in line with our belief in the oneness of humankind. We are told that, when a thought of war enters our minds, we should immediately replace it with a thought of peace. When a feeling of hate begins to take shape in our hearts, we should immediately replace it with a feeling of love. We should do everything possible to overcome our prejudices. Prejudices of race, color, nationality, culture, religion, and sex, these are among the greatest obstacles to building a better world. So many passages in the Bahá'í writings teach us how to walk in the ways of unity and how to help others take the same path. There is a wonderful passage from one of the talks of 'Abdu'l-Bahá, of Whom I will speak later, which I have memorized. He says:
>
> **"Bahá'u'lláh has drawn the circle of unity, He has made a design for the uniting of all the peoples, and for the gathering of them all under the shelter of the tent of universal unity. This is the work of the Divine Bounty, and we must all strive with heart and soul until we have the reality of unity in our midst, and as we work, so will strength be given unto us."** [9]

SECTION 10

The following exercises will help you analyze two aspects of Anna's presentation:

1. In this specific case, Anna chooses to talk first about the subject of God and His Manifestation and then about the principle of unity. She could just as well start her presentation the other way around, beginning with unity, followed by a discussion of God and His Manifestation. Presumably, she chooses the first order because she knows Emilia and finds it a more appropriate sequence of ideas for her. Do you see any advantages in one or the other sequence? Would the order of ideas you choose to present the Faith depend on whom you were teaching? How so? Can you give some examples?

   _____

2. As a side remark during her presentation, Anna expresses the hope that Emilia will become a Bahá'í and conveys the idea that, as a Bahá'í, she will work for the establishment of unity. With which of the statements below do you agree? Mark them.

   _____ It is foolish to invite someone to join the Bahá'í community when he or she still knows little about the Faith. Emilia probably resents the fact that her friend is trying to convert her.

   _____ By expressing the hope that Emilia will become a Bahá'í, Anna oversteps the bounds of moderation and is proselytizing.

   _____ By expressing the hope that her friend will become a Bahá'í, Anna makes it clear, early on, that Emilia is welcome to join the Bahá'í community at any time. But she does this in such a way that Emilia does not feel unduly pressured.

   _____ If we want to recruit people to the Cause, we should not say anything about what they will have to do until after they have drawn close to the Faith. Better yet, we should wait until after they have declared.

_____ It is sad to say, but most people are only interested in what will benefit them. They're not concerned about what they can do to help the world around them. Rather than talking to Emilia about how she will participate in efforts to establish unity if she becomes a Bahá'í, Anna should talk to her about how wonderful it is to be a member of the Bahá'í community and about the love and fellowship one feels when one is part of it.

_____ Anna strikes the right balance in conveying to her friend a sense of what it will mean, in practical terms, for her to become a Bahá'í. She makes it sound challenging, but not overwhelming. The quotation Anna chooses is especially effective, for Emilia understands that she will be strengthened in her efforts to work for the establishment of unity. When Emilia becomes a member of the Bahá'í community, in all probability, she will not be a passive observer, but an active worker for the Cause.

SECTION 11

Like most people today, Emilia is quite attracted to the Bahá'í Teachings on unity. Enthused by the ideas she has heard, she enters into a brief but lively conversation with Anna about the harm that prejudices of every kind bring to humanity. Anna then resumes her presentation:

Bahá'u'lláh was born in 1817 in Ṭihrán, the capital of Iran. From His early childhood, He showed signs of greatness. He received some instruction at home, but did not need to attend school, for He was endowed by God with innate knowledge. Bahá'u'lláh came from a noble family and when he was a young man, was offered a high position in the court of the King, but He refused it. He wished to dedicate His time to helping the oppressed, the sick and the poor, and to champion the cause of justice.

There are two aspects of Bahá'u'lláh's life which I would like to mention in particular. One is the suffering He endured. The other is the tremendous influence He had on the hearts and minds of people. These actually characterize the lives of all the Manifestations of God.

Bahá'u'lláh's sufferings began the moment He arose to proclaim the Cause of God. His life was one of exile, imprisonment and persecution. He was put in chains in a dark and dismal dungeon in Ṭihrán. He was exiled four times from land to land, finally being sent to the Prison City of 'Akká in the Ottoman Empire. So intense were His sufferings there that He has referred to 'Akká as the "Most Great Prison". In one of His Tablets, we read:

"Remember My days during thy days, and My distress and banishment in this remote prison. And be thou so steadfast in My love that thy heart shall not waver, even if the swords of the enemies rain blows upon thee and all the heavens and the earth arise against thee." [10]

I always carry in my bag a small notebook in which I write my favorite passages from the Bahá'í writings. Let me read for you what Bahá'u'lláh has said about His sufferings:

> "**The Ancient Beauty hath consented to be bound with chains that mankind may be released from its bondage, and hath accepted to be made a prisoner within this most mighty Stronghold that the whole world may attain unto true liberty. He hath drained to its dregs the cup of sorrow, that all the peoples of the earth may attain unto abiding joy, and be filled with gladness. This is of the mercy of your Lord, the Compassionate, the Most Merciful. We have accepted to be abased, O believers in the Unity of God, that ye may be exalted, and have suffered manifold afflictions, that ye might prosper and flourish. He Who hath come to build anew the whole world, behold, how they that have joined partners with God have forced Him to dwell within the most desolate of cities!**" [11]

Every effort was made by two powerful courts—those of the King of Iran and the Ottoman Emperor—to oppose Bahá'u'lláh and His Teachings. But the Light of Truth is not easily extinguished. The very water that is poured on this fire to put out its flame turns into oil, and the fire burns with more intensity. Nothing could be done to stop Bahá'u'lláh's growing influence. The farther the authorities banished Him, the greater the number of people who were attracted to His Teachings and recognized His Power and Majesty. In spite of constant persecution, Bahá'u'lláh continued to reveal the Word of God for more than forty years and brought so much love and spiritual energy into this world that the final victory of His Cause is certain.

Bahá'u'lláh passed away in 1892. His Shrine, which we consider the Holiest Spot on earth, is located near the city of 'Akká. Here are some postcards I have of the entrance to the Shrine and the gardens surrounding it. You don't know how much I would like to go on pilgrimage to the Holy Land. I hope, someday, you will be able to do so as well.

SECTION 12

The following exercises explore various aspects of Anna's account of the life of Bahá'u'lláh:

1. In telling the story of the life of Bahá'u'lláh, Anna chooses two main concepts that she wants to get across. In the process, she presents several facts about His life, but clearly it is not her intention to convey a great deal of information. She knows that if, as she hopes, Emilia becomes a Bahá'í, she will study the story of Bahá'u'lláh's life in more detail. What are the two concepts that she is trying to get across?

    a. _____
    b. _____

2. Why do you think she chooses these two concepts?

3. Do you agree with her that these concepts are the two most essential for Emilia to understand at this stage? If not, do you have other suggestions?

4. Make a list of the items of information that Anna gives in her account of Bahá'u'lláh's life.

5. Are there any other facts that you think are necessary to present at this stage?

6. Besides trying to convey two main concepts and some necessary information, Anna is clearly hoping to communicate certain feelings to Emilia. What are these? Does she succeed?

7. Now that you have thought about Anna's presentation of Bahá'u'lláh's life, do you think it would have to be modified if you were speaking to someone of a different religious background? If so, can you give some examples of the changes you would make?

SECTION 13

The reading of Bahá'u'lláh's own words about His sufferings has visibly touched Emilia. She remembers, of course, that Christ gave His life for the salvation of humanity. So Anna and her friend converse for a while about the significance of the sufferings of the Manifestations of God Who, though All-Powerful, willingly accept afflictions so that we may be freed. Anna then asks if it is all right to continue and mentions that she would like to introduce another Central Figure of the Bahá'í Faith, namely, the Báb. She proceeds thus:

Several years before Bahá'u'lláh proclaimed His Mission, God sent a special Messenger to announce His coming. This great Messenger took the title "The Báb" which means the gate. He was indeed a gate to the knowledge of God and to a new era in human existence. For six years He taught ceaselessly that the appearance of the new Manifestation of God was near and prepared the way for His coming. He told the people that they were witnessing the dawn of a new Age, the dawn of the Promised Day of God. He called upon them to purify their hearts from earthly vanities so that they could recognize Him Whom God would soon manifest.

Thousands upon thousands of people accepted the Message of the Báb and began to follow His Teachings. But the government of Iran and the powerful clergy who ruled over the masses rose against Him. His followers were persecuted and large numbers were put to death. The Báb Himself at the age of 31 was martyred by a regiment of soldiers who, at the orders of the government, suspended Him in a public square and opened fire on Him.

So that you can see how penetrating the Words of the Báb are I would like to recite to you two of His prayers:

"Is there any Remover of difficulties save God? Say: Praised be God! He is God! All are His servants, and all abide by His bidding!" [12]

"Say: God sufficeth all things above all things, and nothing in the heavens or in the earth but God sufficeth. Verily, He is in Himself the Knower, the Sustainer, the Omnipotent." [13]

Many Bahá'ís know especially the first prayer by heart and say it aloud or mentally in times of difficulties. If you want, we can pause a little and you can memorize it. It is really easy to do so.

After the memorization, Anna continues:

Following His martyrdom, the remains of the Báb were recovered by His followers and taken from place to place, always hidden from the enemies of the Faith. Finally they were transferred to Mount Carmel in the Holy Land. Here, I have some postcards that I would like to show you of His Shrine in Haifa and a few other Holy Places in that city and in 'Akká, which is across the bay. These twin cities are today the spiritual and administrative world center of the Bahá'í Faith—the spiritual center because it is here that the Shrines of the Báb and Bahá'u'lláh, as well as many other Holy Places, are located, and the administrative center because the Seat of the supreme governing body of the Faith, the Universal House of Justice, is also on Mount Carmel.

SECTION 14

The exercises below will help you think about this part of Anna's presentation.

1. Make a list of the important concepts and items of information Anna conveys in her account of the Báb's life.

Concepts:

_____
_____
_____
_____
_____
_____
_____
_____
_____
_____
_____
_____
_____
_____

Information:

_____
_____
_____
_____
_____
_____
_____
_____
_____
_____

2. Why is it important to introduce the Figure of the Báb at an early stage in a presentation of the Faith like the one Anna is making? _____

_____
_____
_____
_____
_____

SECTION 15

Having completed her presentation on the Twin Manifestations, Anna proceeds to speak about 'Abdu'l-Bahá and the Covenant of Bahá'u'lláh:

The idea most central to our lives as Bahá'ís is that we have entered into a Covenant with Bahá'u'lláh. As you know, in all other religions, after the passing of the Manifestation, His followers had thousands of disputes among themselves and, as a result, split the religion into many sects. The cause of disunity was sometimes the desire for leadership of certain ambitious individuals. But, when differences of opinion arose between even sincere believers about what the Words of the Manifestation meant, no one had been authorized by the Manifestation Himself to settle the disagreements, and this contributed to conflict and dissension. Each set of interpretations led to the creation of a different sect.

Bahá'u'lláh has protected His Faith against such division by endowing it with a unique power, the power of the Covenant. Before His passing, He stated in the clearest terms, in writing, that after Him, all Bahá'ís should turn to 'Abdu'l-Bahá. 'Abdu'l-Bahá, His oldest Son, was thus named the sole Interpreter of His Words and the Center of His Covenant. He had been raised by Bahá'u'lláh Himself, had recognized His Station even as a child, and had shared the sufferings of His Father. He was a most precious gift given to humanity, the perfect Exemplar of all Bahá'í Teachings.

'Abdu'l-Bahá lived on this earth for 77 years. He was born on the same night the Báb declared His Mission in 1844 and passed away in November 1921. His life was filled with affliction, but to everyone who entered His presence He brought the greatest joy and happiness. After the passing of His Father, the responsibility for the Bahá'í community fell on His shoulders, and He labored day and night to spread the Faith throughout the East and the West. He wrote thousands of Tablets to individuals and groups everywhere and clarified the Teachings of His Father. His interpretations are now an essential part of the Writings of the Bahá'í Faith.

By focusing on 'Abdu'l-Bahá as the Center of Bahá'u'lláh's Covenant, the Bahá'ís of the world remain united in their efforts to live a Bahá'í life and to create a new civilization. We remember that as part of our promise to Bahá'u'lláh, we are to love one another and, in 'Abdu'l-Bahá, we see the perfect example of one who loves. We remember that we must uphold justice, that we must be generous, that we must overlook the faults of others, and from the example of 'Abdu'l-Bahá we learn justice, generosity and forgiveness. More than anything else, by keeping our focus on 'Abdu'l-Bahá, we are always aware of our covenant with Bahá'u'lláh that we will not allow the unity of His followers to be broken and that, united as a worldwide community, we will labor until the oneness of humankind has been firmly established.

In His Will and Testament, 'Abdu'l-Bahá named His grandson the Guardian of the Faith and after His passing, Shoghi Effendi became the authorized interpreter of the Teachings. For 36 years, he continued the work of His Grandfather, clarifying the Words of the Manifestation and firmly establishing His Faith in all parts of the planet. Five and a half years after his passing, the Bahá'ís of the world elected the Universal House of Justice, as envisioned by Bahá'u'lláh and clearly described by 'Abdu'l-Bahá and the Guardian. The Universal House of Justice is the supreme institution of the Faith to which all the Bahá'ís of the world now turn.

SECTION 16

You probably noted that this part of Anna's presentation is weighty, because she explains to Emilia in a few words some extremely profound concepts. The exercise below will help you examine her remarks in more detail.

1. Up to this point, Anna has, in keeping with the statement of the Universal House of Justice, spoken to Emilia about the Station of the Forerunner of the Faith, the Báb, and its Author, Bahá'u'lláh. She now wants to help Emilia recognize the Station of 'Abdu'l-Bahá. To do this, Anna also introduces the concept of the Covenant of Bahá'u'lláh. She presents a number of facts in order to assist Emilia in gaining some understanding of these two interrelated concepts.

   Below is a list of some of these facts. Each statement is intended to contribute to Emilia's understanding of one or the other of these two concepts, or both. Put a "1" in front of those that you feel largely reinforce the concept of the Station of 'Abdu'l-Bahá and a "2" in front of those that are more directed towards the concept of the Covenant of Bahá'u'lláh. If you feel the statement contributes equally to the understanding of both concepts, put a "1" and "2" next to it.

   _____ All other religions have been divided into numerous sects because of the lack of an explicitly authorized interpreter.

   _____ 'Abdu'l-Bahá is the Center of Bahá'u'lláh's Covenant.

   _____ 'Abdu'l-Bahá is the Interpreter of Bahá'u'lláh's Words.

   _____ The establishment of the Universal House of Justice was envisioned by Bahá'u'lláh.

   _____ 'Abdu'l-Bahá named His grandson the Guardian of the Faith in His Will and Testament.

   _____ 'Abdu'l-Bahá wrote thousands of Tablets clarifying the Teachings of the Faith.

   _____ Bahá'u'lláh protected His Faith from division by endowing it with the power of the Covenant.

   _____ 'Abdu'l-Bahá is the Perfect Exemplar of Bahá'u'lláh's Teachings.

   _____ 'Abdu'l-Bahá brought joy and happiness to everyone who entered His presence.

_____ Bahá'u'lláh stated in the clearest terms, in writing, that, after His passing, all Bahá'ís should turn to 'Abdu'l-Bahá.

_____ The desire for leadership can be the cause of disunity in a religion.

_____ 'Abdu'l-Bahá labored day and night to spread the Faith throughout the East and the West.

_____ The Bahá'ís of the world elected the Universal House of Justice soon after the passing of the Guardian.

_____ The lack of an authorized interpreter in a religion opens the door to conflict and dissension.

SECTION 17

During her explanation of the Covenant of Bahá'u'lláh and the Station of 'Abdu'l-Bahá, Anna notices that Emilia is somewhat overwhelmed. She quickly weighs in her mind the two choices before her: she can take time and discuss the subject in much more depth, or continue with her presentation and make sure that in another conversation soon they would study the theme of the Covenant again. She decides on the second course of action and continues thus:

Many of the ideas I have explained on this last subject require a great deal of thought. If you agree, some other time we can discuss this matter in more depth. For that discussion, I will bring a few passages from Bahá'u'lláh's Book of the Covenant as well as the Will and Testament of 'Abdu'l-Bahá so we can read them together. But let me go on and present to you a few other ideas you will want to know about the Bahá'í Faith right from the beginning.

Emilia agrees and graciously states that she actually liked the explanation, that she has gotten a glimpse of the importance of Bahá'u'lláh's Covenant, and that she looks forward to studying the subject soon. Anna, happy and relaxed, continues:

A most important aspect of every religion is the laws that the Manifestation brings to humanity in order to guide it in the right path. Some of these laws and commandments are eternal, others change as humanity progresses and evolves. In the Faith we are taught that we should not think of Bahá'í laws as a series of do's and don'ts. Bahá'u'lláh tells us that His laws are **"the lamps of My loving providence among My servants, and the keys of My mercy for My creatures."** [3] Nor should we obey these laws out of fear of punishment, for He clearly has stated in His Most Holy Book: **"Observe My commandments, for the love of My beauty."** [14]

These ideas will become clearer if I give you a few examples of Bahá'í laws. In the physical world, human beings have to eat every day. This is a requirement of the human body; if we don't, we will get sick and quickly die. We can say, then, that eating daily is a law of physical existence which has to be obeyed. In the same way one of the commandments of Bahá'u'lláh is that we should pray every day. Like our body, our soul needs constant nourishment, and prayer provides the nourishment for our spiritual growth. There are many beautiful prayers revealed by the Báb, by Bahá'u'lláh and by 'Abdu'l-Bahá which we can say when we are alone or recite in meetings. Some of these prayers are special, and some are obligatory. One obligatory prayer is recited by Bahá'ís every day sometime between noon and sunset. It says:

> **"I bear witness, O my God, that Thou hast created me to know Thee and to worship Thee. I testify, at this moment, to my powerlessness and to Thy might, to my poverty and to Thy wealth.**
>
> **"There is none other God but Thee, the Help in Peril, the Self-Subsisting."** [15]

It is a short and beautiful prayer and having seen how easy it is for you to memorize verses, I am sure you will know it by heart after repeating it a few times.

In another commandment, Bahá'u'lláh prohibits backbiting and calumny. This is important because, if you think about it, one of the greatest enemies of unity is backbiting. And unfortunately, it has become an established practice among most of humanity to talk about other people's faults in their absence. Everybody seems to be concerned with everybody else's shortcomings, which are made bigger and bigger as they are constantly mentioned. 'Abdu'l-Bahá tells us to do just the opposite. If we see ten good qualities in someone and one fault, we should concentrate on the ten, and even if a person has ten faults and only one good quality we should focus on that one quality.

Emilia, who is listening with special interest to Anna's last comments, remembers some recent incidents at school in which backbiting resulted in many people being hurt. The two friends talk for some time about how gossip can destroy a friendship and then Anna searches in her notebook and reads the following:

> **"O Companion of My Throne! Hear no evil, and see no evil, abase not thyself, neither sigh and weep. Speak no evil, that thou mayest not hear it spoken unto thee, and magnify not the faults of others that thine own faults may not appear great; and wish not the abasement of anyone, that thine own abasement be not exposed. Live then the days of thy life, that are less than a fleeting moment, with thy mind stainless, thy heart unsullied, thy thoughts pure, and thy nature sanctified, so that, free and content, thou mayest put away this mortal frame, and repair unto the mystic paradise and abide in the eternal kingdom forevermore."** [16]

Then Anna continues:

> Although this does not affect us much at our age, you should also know that Bahá'u'lláh prohibits the drinking of alcohol and, of course, substance abuse. Drinking alcohol is really one of the greatest social ills that exists today in the world. It is one of the most common causes of violence and the ruin of healthy family life. To tell you the truth, I have never understood why people would take

something that interferes with their minds and makes them lose their ability to think clearly. Drinking makes people capable of acting in shameful ways, when we have actually been created noble. I know a beautiful quote from Bahá'u'lláh's Writings about nobility:

> **"O Son of Spirit! I created thee rich, why dost thou bring thyself down to poverty? Noble I made thee, wherewith dost thou abase thyself? Out of the essence of knowledge I gave thee being, why seekest thou enlightenment from anyone beside Me? Out of the clay of love I molded thee, how dost thou busy thyself with another? Turn thy sight unto thyself, that thou mayest find Me standing within thee, mighty, powerful and self-subsisting."** [17]

Another commandment of Bahá'u'lláh, which is one of my favorites, is about the obligation of parents and society to educate children. Here, I have in my notebook a short passage from 'Abdu'l-Bahá's Writings that explains this well:

> **"Therefore, the beloved of God and the maid-servants of the Merciful must train their children with life and heart and teach them in the school of virtue and perfection. They must not be lax in this matter; they must not be inefficient. Truly, if a babe did not live at all it were better than to let it grow ignorant, for that innocent babe, in later life, would become afflicted with innumerable defects, responsible to and questioned by God, reproached and rejected by the people. What a sin this would be and what an omission!**
>
> **"The first duty of the beloved of God and the maid-servants of the Merciful is this: They must strive by all possible means to educate both sexes, male and female; girls like boys; there is no difference whatsoever between them. The ignorance of both is blameworthy, and negligence in both cases is reprovable. 'Are they who know and they who do not know equal?'"** [18]

You know, after I reflected on this great commandment, I decided to do something about it. So I hold a Bahá'í children's class with a friend once every week and we have seventeen students. I would love to invite you to come and help us with our class. Do you have time this Saturday afternoon?

SECTION 18

To help you think about this portion of Anna's presentation, complete the exercises below.

1. In this part of her presentation, Anna is trying to follow the guidance of the Universal House of Justice to inform the seeker of the existence of laws in the Faith that must be followed. With which of the statements below do you agree?

    _____ At this stage, it would be better for Anna not to bring up the question of laws at all. In today's society, people value their own personal freedom and the idea of "religious laws" turns them off.

110 - The Act of Teaching

_____ Anna should mention most, if not all, of the Bahá'í laws to Emilia, for example, the laws of inheritance, marriage, burial, and Ḥuqúqu'lláh. Otherwise Emilia will not be fully informed of what it means to be a Bahá'í.

_____ What is most important is for Emilia to understand the fact that laws exist in the Bahá'í Faith, to have some idea of the nature of these laws, and to be aware that, as a Bahá'í, she will have to obey them. At this stage, she does not need to know what all the laws are.

_____ For Anna's purposes, it would be sufficient to give an example of one law, that is, the law of prayer. She overdoes it by presenting four.

_____ Anna's explanation of the law of prayer is very effective. By first presenting one of the laws governing the physical world, Anna is able to explain to Emilia the meaning of "laws" and helps her move away from the notion of do's and don'ts.

_____ Talking to a seeker about Bahá'u'lláh's prohibition of the use of alcohol is not a good idea, especially with a young person who is struggling to gain her own identity and show she is becoming an adult. She will naturally want to try drinking alcohol, and any mention of a law against it will only push her away from the Faith.

_____ The way Anna presents Bahá'u'lláh's prohibition of the use of alcohol is appropriate. By talking about the effects of alcohol on one's clarity of mind, she shows the wisdom of the law. Moreover, by introducing the subject of nobility, she places the law in a higher, spiritual context.

_____ Anna makes a mistake by not talking much more firmly about obedience to Bahá'u'lláh's laws. In fact, she should bring up the question of administrative sanctions so that Emilia knows what the consequences of disobedience are.

_____ While not pressing the point about obedience to Bahá'u'lláh's laws, Anna clearly conveys to Emilia the idea that obedience flows from the love of God and not from fear of punishment. When Emilia becomes a Bahá'í, obeying the laws will be a natural consequence of her love for Bahá'u'lláh.

_____ If you were teaching someone who has a drinking problem, it would be most important for you to explain to him the law prohibiting the use of alcohol. In this case, of course, you would have to tell him that if he becomes a Bahá'í, he would have to stop drinking immediately.

_____ If you were teaching someone who has a drinking problem, it would be most important for you to explain to him the law prohibiting the use of alcohol. Recognizing his problem, however, you could explain to him that it would be all right for him to go ahead and continue to drink after becoming a Bahá'í, so long as no one sees him.

_____ If you were teaching someone who has a drinking problem, it would be important for you to explain to him Bahá'u'lláh's prohibition of the use of alcohol, along with the other laws. You would also mention to him that it is not always easy to follow every law; we are not perfect and sometimes we make mistakes. But when we accept Bahá'u'lláh, and as we pray to Him, He Himself helps us to overcome our weaknesses and gives us strength to obey His laws.

2. Suppose you are teaching someone who has difficulty believing in God. Would you still present to him or her the law of prayer? If so, how would you do it?

_____
_____
_____
_____
_____
_____
_____
_____
_____
_____
_____
_____
_____
_____

SECTION 19

Anna's first conversation with Emilia about the Faith is coming to a close. Emilia has shown great interest throughout the presentation, and this has encouraged Anna to explain certain ideas in relative detail. Now she must conclude her introductory remarks:

I am sure you are aware that I am inviting you to join a religion and not just accept a collection of nice ideals. In fact, the Bahá'í Faith is a very organized religion whose aim is nothing less than the unification of the entire human race. It will be helpful for you to think of the work of the Bahá'ís as the building of a world civilization. The Universal House of Justice tells us that there are three participants in this work, each with a very important role.

The first participant is the individual believer. It is the duty of this individual to remain firm in the Covenant, to strive daily to bring his or her life in line with Bahá'u'lláh's Teachings, and to serve humanity, always conscious of the fact that life does not end with death and that one's relation with God is eternal. After death, our souls become free and continue to progress towards God for all eternity. Our lives here are very much like the life of an infant in the womb of the mother. For some nine months the child develops faculties—eyes, ears, hands and so on—to be used later in this world. In the same way, we are to develop here the spiritual faculties that we need to progress in the other worlds of God. Of course, we do not achieve our purpose by just thinking about it. We have to work, serve our fellow human beings, and share the knowledge we gain with others.

The second participant is the community. Human beings were not created to exist alone. We live in communities and must work together to build the new civilization. The community closest to us is the local one which consists of the Bahá'ís of our village or town. It is in the local community where we learn to cooperate with one another, to grow together and become united. In addition to being members of the local community, we are also members of the national community and then the worldwide Bahá'í community which is constantly expanding and attracting people from every religious background, race, and nationality.

The institutions of the Faith, the Universal House of Justice tells us, represent the third participant in the building of the new civilization. This is a subject about which we will have to talk some more when we discuss the Covenant. For now, let me just mention that included in the commandments of Bahá'u'lláh are many related to the way society should be organized. In the past, the Manifestations of God have not said much about how their followers should organize themselves and people have had to discover how to do this by themselves. But, in the case of the Bahá'í Faith, Bahá'u'lláh has brought His own Administrative Order, which means that He has told us what institutions we must create, how they should function, and how humanity should be governed.

We have already spoken about the supreme institution, which is the Universal House of Justice. In each country, Bahá'ís elect once a year the National Spiritual Assembly, and in each locality, the Local Spiritual Assembly. This is the institution that you will get to know the soonest. There are no priests or clergy in the Bahá'í Faith, and it is the Local Spiritual Assembly that guides the affairs of the community and watches over the well-being of the individual believers. A Local Spiritual Assembly consists of nine members elected in a prayerful atmosphere by secret ballot by all the adult believers in the community. Spiritual Assemblies are extremely important to Bahá'ís. Through them we learn how human affairs are to be administered and how a new order can be established in society, an order which is to be known as the World Order of Bahá'u'lláh.

We can imagine that the conversation between Anna and Emilia comes to a close here. Emilia is clearly eager to continue the discussion another day. Anna takes a small prayer book out of her bag and gives it to Emilia as a gift, suggesting they say a prayer together before they go their separate ways. Emilia opens the book and reads:

"O God! Refresh and gladden my spirit. Purify my heart. Illumine my powers. I lay all my affairs in Thy hand. Thou art my Guide and my Refuge. I will no longer be sorrowful and grieved; I will be a happy and joyful being. O God! I will no longer be full of anxiety, nor will I let trouble harass me. I will not dwell on the unpleasant things of life.

"O God! Thou art more friend to me than I am to myself. I dedicate myself to Thee, O Lord." [19]

Although the account we have related of Anna and Emilia is not a real one, it is based on the experience of thousands of Bahá'ís around the world. As an end to the story, then, we can confidently say that, in a few days and after one or two more conversations, Emilia will join the Bahá'í community.

SECTION 20

Let us examine Anna's overall presentation through the following two exercises:

1. Anna's remarks, as especially brought into focus by the concluding ones, will form the basis for Emilia's perception of her responsibilities as an individual believer, of her participation in the work of the community, and of her future relationship with the institutions of the Faith.

   What image of the individual believer is Anna trying to convey? What are some of the characteristics of this individual? _____

   What image of the Bahá'í community is Anna trying to convey? What are some of its characteristics? _____

   What image of the institutions of the Faith is Anna trying to convey? What are some of their characteristics? _____

_____

_____

_____

_____

_____

2. Throughout, Anna is clearly trying to help Emilia accept the Bahá'í Faith. Which of the following would you consider the main thrust of her appeal?

_____ That Bahá'ís are nice people and the Bahá'í community is united, therefore you should join us.

_____ That the Bahá'í Faith contains the most progressive spiritual and social principles and since you accept them, you are a Bahá'í.

_____ That with the short introduction I have given you, you now need to make a thorough study of the Bahá'í Faith and then decide whether or not to become a Bahá'í.

_____ That on the basis of what I have said, and some further explanation I will give you, you will come to see that Bahá'u'lláh is the Manifestation of God for today and feel the desire to become one of His devoted followers.

SECTION 21

In examining the act of teaching, we have considered thus far the role of proclamation, the ability to recognize receptive souls, and several characteristics of the content of the message we should convey to those we teach. We are also aware that we carry out our duty to teach in at least two contexts: in our own personal teaching plans and in projects organized by our institutions. At this point, let us explore these two contexts in a little more detail, beginning with systematic personal teaching plans. You are already familiar with the quotation below from your study of earlier courses, but are now asked to reflect on its meaning more closely, for it provides the basic elements of every personal teaching plan.

> "O wayfarer in the path of God! Take thou thy portion of the ocean of His grace, and deprive not thyself of the things that lie hidden in its depths. Be thou of them that have partaken of its treasures. A dewdrop out of this ocean would, if shed upon all that are in the heavens and on the earth, suffice to enrich them with the bounty of God, the Almighty, the All-Knowing, the All-Wise. With the hands of renunciation draw forth from its life-giving waters, and sprinkle therewith all created things, that they may be cleansed from all man-made limitations and may approach the mighty seat of God, this hallowed and resplendent Spot.
>
> "Be not grieved if thou performest it thyself alone. Let God be all-sufficient for thee. Commune intimately with His Spirit, and be thou of the thankful.

Proclaim the Cause of thy Lord unto all who are in the heavens and on the earth. Should any man respond to thy call, lay bare before him the pearls of the wisdom of the Lord, thy God, which His Spirit hath sent down unto thee, and be thou of them that truly believe. And should any one reject thine offer, turn thou away from him, and put thy trust and confidence in the Lord, thy God, the Lord of all worlds." [20]

1. Complete the following sentences:

    a. We should take our _____ of the ocean of _____.

    b. With the hands of _____, we should draw forth from its _____.

    c. We are to sprinkle _____ with the life-giving waters of God's grace.

    d. We should not be _____ if we must perform this task _____.

    e. We should _____ with His Spirit.

    f. We are to be of the _____.

    g. We should _____ the Cause of our Lord unto all who are in the heavens and on the earth.

    h. Should any person respond to our call, we should _____ before him the _____ of the Lord.

    i. Should any person reject our offer, we should _____ from him, and put our _____ in God.

2. What does it mean that we should take our portion of the ocean of God's grace?
    _____
    _____
    _____

3. What are some of the things that lie hidden in the depths of this ocean and which, if discovered, would enable us to become effective teachers of the Cause? ____
    _____
    _____
    _____

4. What can a single drop of the ocean of God's grace do? _____
   _____
   _____

5. Why must we use "hands of renunciation" to draw forth from the life-giving waters of this ocean? _____
   _____
   _____

6. What should we do with the waters we draw forth from the ocean of God's grace?
   _____

7. What effect will this sprinkling have? _____
   _____
   _____
   _____

8. Do we always have to teach the Faith with the help of other Bahá'ís? _____

9. Do we need anyone except God when we proclaim and teach the Cause? _____

10. With whom should we commune when we proclaim and teach the Cause? _____

11. For what should we be thankful when we proclaim and teach the Cause? _____
    _____
    _____
    _____
    _____

12. To whom should we proclaim the Cause? _____
    _____

13. Whom should we teach? _____

14. What should we do if the Message we give is rejected? _____
    _____

15. Does the fact that we should turn away from those who reject the Message mean that we should not be friends with them anymore? Or does it simply mean that we should not insist on talking to them about the Faith? _____
    _____
    _____

The Act of Teaching - 117

16. Below are a few phrases about teaching. Decide which ones are most in keeping with the above passage from the Writings of Bahá'u'lláh. Mark them.

_____ I decided that the person I should teach is my best friend, Miguel. So for the past five years, I have been concentrating my efforts only on him. He is not responding well, but someday he will. Basically, that is my personal teaching plan.

_____ I think that it is our responsibility to proclaim the Faith to people. Then it is their business whether they wish to investigate it further. If they really want, they ask for a book to read so that they can decide for themselves.

_____ Yesterday, I was explaining Bahá'u'lláh's Message to one of my neighbors while we were having a cup of coffee together. After a while she said that, although she respected my enthusiasm, she was happy with her own religion. But she said it in such a way that it was clear she was not closing the door to future conversations about the Faith. So when we are next together, I will try to explain that there is no need to reject one's own religion, but that all things, including religion, have to be made new.

_____ Just because someone tells me that they are not interested in hearing about the Faith, doesn't mean that it is necessarily so. I just insist.

_____ If a person knows that I am a Bahá'í but does not ask me any questions about the Faith, it means he or she is not interested.

_____ I try to meet as many people as possible and, when occasions arise, I tell them something about the Faith. If I find them receptive, I continue to teach them until I can finally invite them to join the Faith.

SECTION 22

The passage from the Writings of Bahá'u'lláh which we have just studied is clearly a call to every individual believer to arise and teach. But it goes further to provide us with certain steps we are to take as we discharge this sacred duty. With this passage in mind, you are now asked to focus your attention on devising your own systematic personal teaching plan. What would some of the elements of such a plan be? Carrying out the exercises below will help you to identify elements of your plan. As you do so, think of your own life and respond according to your own personal circumstances.

1. Clearly a crucial element of your personal teaching plan is your unshakable resolve to make concrete efforts in your daily life to find receptive souls and to teach them. Whenever we make a firm commitment to do something, our resolve is tested. Obstacles inevitably arise. In the case of teaching, some of the obstacles put in our path come from opposition to the Faith or the condition of the world around us. For example, materialism in society can make our efforts to teach more difficult, as can the general apathy of people towards spiritual matters. What are

some of the obstacles arising from the condition of the world that you are likely to encounter as you set out to teach?

a. _____

b. _____

c. _____

d. _____

e. _____

f. _____

Unfortunately, it is also possible for our teaching efforts to be hindered by our own friends, even Bahá'ís, who, without realizing it, discourage us from pursuing our goals. For example, the pessimism of those who, for whatever reason, have not been successful in teaching and the prejudices of some towards a particular group of people can become obstacles in our path. Mention a few other such obstacles:

a. _____

b. _____

c. _____

d. _____

e. _____

f. _____

2. Having resolved to arise and teach the Faith, you will need to think about your situation and the circumstances of your own life. On that basis, you will figure out the teaching possibilities that these circumstances offer you. Write a short paragraph about your situation in life, for instance, what your occupation is, where you live, what kind of people you meet, what your resources are, and so on:

_____

_____

_____

_____

_____

_____

_____

_____

With the above in mind, write down the various possibilities that exist in your life for systematic teaching:

_____
_____
_____
_____
_____
_____
_____
_____
_____
_____
_____
_____

3. In the passage you studied in the preceding lesson, you are called upon to proclaim the Faith to as many people as possible—to "sprinkle" all created things with the "life-giving waters" drawn forth from the "ocean of His grace". Thus, as another element of your personal teaching plan, you will need to devise various ways in which you can constantly meet new people, some of whom will prove to be receptive to Bahá'u'lláh's Message. For example, you could join an organization whose aims are in harmony with the Teachings. If you live near an educational center, you could attend lectures on subjects such as moral development, the advancement of women, and comparative religion. This element of your plan is extremely important, because if you do not constantly meet new people, you will end up focusing all your attention on the same few individuals year after year—most of whom may not even be receptive. Write down some of the ways you can come in contact with more and more people:

_____
_____
_____
_____
_____
_____
_____
_____

4. As you come in contact with an increasing number of people, you will proclaim the Faith to them in a wise and dignified manner. On the basis of your comments above, think of the kinds of people you will meet and how you will go about making

the aims of Bahá'u'lláh's Revelation known to them. Clearly, you will merely be able to put down your initial ideas, since you will only know with certainty what to tell people when you are in the actual situation. Furthermore, your ideas will change as you gain experience and proclaim the Faith to more and more people in a various situations.

5. While you continue to proclaim the Faith to more and more people, letting them know that you are a Bahá'í through both words and deeds, and giving them glimpses of the beauty of the Teachings, you will start to teach those who respond to you. Depending on their degree of receptivity, you will decide to use the direct or indirect method. With either method, your aim will be to help them understand the significance of Bahá'u'lláh's Message and decide to join the ranks of His followers. From your study of the third unit of Book 2, "Introducing Bahá'í Beliefs", you know how to go about teaching different aspects of the Faith through the indirect method, and the earlier sections in this unit have given you an example of direct teaching. Keeping in mind the groups of people you identified above, make a list of the things you will do to teach those who respond to your proclamation efforts. For example, you may decide to hold regular firesides. You will also continually turn to God, asking Him to confirm your teaching endeavors.

6. When a person joins the Bahá'í community, it does not necessarily mean that he or she understands a great deal about the Faith and can withstand tests alone and unaided. Often a person becomes a Bahá'í because of a strong feeling in his or her heart that Bahá'u'lláh is, indeed, the Manifestation of God for today. Newly enrolled believers have to be nurtured so that the spark of faith that has been lit in their hearts is not put out by the first contrary wind. List the things that you will do to nurture those you aid to recognize Bahá'u'lláh, helping them to become strong and confirmed believers, able to stand on their own, and eager to dedicate their energies to the teaching of others.

SECTION 23

In *The Advent of Divine Justice*, the Guardian has written a passage in which he eloquently describes the basic elements of a systematic personal teaching plan. The passage has been divided in short sections below. Read each one and then fill in the blanks in the sentences that follow.

> "Having on his own initiative, and undaunted by any hindrances with which either friend or foe may, unwittingly or deliberately, obstruct his path, resolved to arise and respond to the call of teaching, let him carefully consider every avenue of approach which he might utilize in his personal attempts to capture the attention, maintain the interest, and deepen the faith, of those whom he seeks to bring into the fold of his Faith. Let him survey the possibilities which the particular circumstances in which he lives offer him, evaluate their advantages, and proceed intelligently and systematically to utilize them for the achievement of the object he has in mind." [21]

1. The Guardian tells us that we should, on our own _____, resolve to _____ and _____ to the call of _____.

2. In so doing, we are not to allow the obstacles that either _____ or _____ may, _____ or _____, put in our path to divert us from our intention.

3. Firm in our resolve, we should carefully consider _____ _____ of _____ which we might use in our personal efforts to catch the _____, maintain the _____, and deepen the _____ of those whom we seek to teach the Faith.

4. Firm in our resolve, we should carefully _____ every avenue of approach which we might _____ in our personal efforts to _____ the attention, _____ the interest, and _____ the faith of those whom we seek to teach the Faith.

The Act of Teaching - 123

5. We are told to _____ the possibilities which the particular _____ in which we live offer us.

6. We should _____ the advantages of the possibilities before us.

7. Having done so, we should proceed _____ and _____ to _____ them as a means for teaching the Faith.

"Let him also attempt to devise such methods as association with clubs, exhibitions, and societies, lectures on subjects akin to the teachings and ideals of his Cause such as temperance, morality, social welfare, religious and racial tolerance, economic cooperation, Islám, and comparative religion, or participation in social, cultural, humanitarian, charitable, and educational organizations and enterprises which, while safeguarding the integrity of his Faith, will open up to him a multitude of ways and means whereby he can enlist successively the sympathy, the support, and ultimately the allegiance of those with whom he comes in contact." [22]

8. We should also try to think of such ways as association with _____, _____, and _____, and _____ on subjects in harmony with the _____ and _____ of the Cause.

9. Moreover, we should try find ways of participating in _____, _____, _____, _____, and _____ and _____, while always _____ the integrity of the Faith.

10. This we should do so that a multitude of _____ and _____ will open up to us whereby we can enlist the _____, the _____, and ultimately the _____ of those with whom we come in contact.

"Let him, while such contacts are being made, bear in mind the claims which his Faith is constantly making upon him to preserve its dignity, and station, to safeguard the integrity of its laws and principles, to demonstrate its comprehensiveness and universality, and to defend fearlessly its manifold and vital interests. Let him consider the degree of his hearer's receptivity, and decide for himself the suitability of either the direct or indirect method of teaching, whereby he can impress upon the seeker the vital importance of the Divine Message, and persuade him to throw in his lot with those who have already embraced it." [23]

11. While we are making such contacts, we should never forget our responsibility to _____ the dignity of the Faith, to _____ the integrity of its _____ and _____, to _____ its comprehensiveness and _____, and to _____ fearlessly its many vital _____.

12. The Guardian tells us that we should consider the degree of our listener's _____, and decide for ourselves the _____ of either the _____ or _____ method of teaching.

13. In choosing either method, we should remember that our aim is to _____ upon the seeker the _____ of the Divine Message and _____ him to _____ with those who have already embraced it.

"Let him remember the example set by 'Abdu'l-Bahá, and His constant admonition to shower such kindness upon the seeker, and exemplify to such a degree the spirit of the teachings he hopes to instill into him, that the recipient will be spontaneously impelled to identify himself with the Cause embodying such teachings. Let him refrain, at the outset, from insisting on such laws and observances as might impose too severe a strain on the seeker's newly awakened faith, and endeavor to nurse him, patiently, tactfully, and yet determinedly, into full maturity, and aid him to proclaim his unqualified acceptance of whatever has been ordained by Bahá'u'lláh." [24]

14. In our teaching efforts, we should call to mind the _____ set by 'Abdu'l-Bahá and His constant admonition to _____ the seeker with _____ and to strive to _____ the _____ of the teachings we hope to instill in him.

15. We should be so vigilant in following 'Abdu'l-Bahá's example that the seeker will be _____ to identify himself with the Cause.

16. Having drawn the seeker to the Faith, we should be careful at the beginning not to _____ on such _____ and _____ as might _____ on his newly awakened faith.

The Act of Teaching - 125

17. We are to _____ him, patiently, tactfully and yet determinedly, into _____, and _____ him to proclaim his _____ of whatever has been _____ by Bahá'u'lláh.

18. We are to nurse him, _____, _____ and yet _____, into full maturity, and aid him to _____ his unqualified acceptance of whatever has been ordained by Bahá'u'lláh.

"Let him, as soon as that stage has been attained, introduce him to the body of his fellow-believers, and seek, through constant fellowship and active participation in the local activities of his community, to enable him to contribute his share to the enrichment of its life, the furtherance of its tasks, the consolidations of its interests, and the coordination of its activities with those of its sister communities." 25

19. As soon as the seeker has reached this stage, we should _____ him to the other members of the community.

20. From that point forward we should seek, through _____ _____ and _____ in the _____ of the community, to enable him to _____ his share to the _____ _____ of its life, the _____ of its tasks, the _____ of its interests, and the _____ of its joint activities with other communities.

"Let him not be content until he has infused into his spiritual child so deep a longing as to impel him to arise independently, in his turn, and devote his energies to the quickening of other souls, and the upholding of the laws and principles laid down by his newly adopted Faith." 26

21. The Guardian tells us that we should not be content until we have _____ in those we teach so deep a _____ as to _____ them to arise _____ and _____ their _____ to the teaching of other souls and the upholding of the laws and principles of the Faith.

126 - The Act of Teaching

SECTION 24

Having identified the elements of a personal teaching plan, you may now wish to make an initial plan of action for a certain period of time, either several weeks or a few months. Your plan will be most helpful if it is specific, mentioning the names of people you know and indicating definite things you intend to do. As you pursue your plan, then, fresh opportunities will arise and relationships will develop, and you will devise new steps accordingly.

SECTION 25

Essential as they are, personal teaching plans are not sufficient by themselves as a means for bringing vast numbers of people into the Faith. Therefore, as we have said often in these units, whether individually or in groups, we participate wholeheartedly in the teaching projects devised by our communities and institutions. It is unfortunately true that, from time to time, the believers in some communities end up arguing with one another over the merits of personal teaching plans as opposed to collective teaching endeavors. A few even go so far as to say that organized projects and campaigns, especially those designed to enroll large numbers, are undesirable, convinced that the only appropriate means of teaching is through individual efforts. Such arguments are unproductive and simply paralyze all teaching. Remembering that the two approaches are complementary and that both are essential for the growth of the Faith, you will always be in a position to contribute to unity of thought on this vital matter in your community.

Below are but a few of the many quotations from the writings of the Guardian that demonstrate unequivocally the necessity of systematic teaching planned by the institutions of the Faith. In October 1935, when the building of the machinery of the Bahá'í Administrative Order in North America had sufficiently advanced, the Guardian cabled the following message to the believers there:

> "A new hour has struck in history of our beloved Cause, calling for nationwide, systematic, sustained efforts in teaching field, enabling thereby these forces to be directed into such channels as shall redound to the glory of our Faith and to the honor of its institutions." [27]

Some months later, in May 1936, he wrote to those same believers:

> "A systematic, carefully conceived, and well-established plan should be devised, vigorously pursued and continuously extended." [28]

And in March 1945, he told them:

> "Above all, the healing Message of Bahá'u'lláh must during the opening years of the second Bahá'í century, and through the instrumentality of an already properly functioning Administrative Order, whose ramifications have been extended to the four corners of the Western Hemisphere, be vividly, systematically brought to the attention of the masses, in their hour of grief, misery and confusion." [29]

The Universal House of Justice has often commented on the relationship between individual initiative in teaching and collective endeavors in this field. In its 1979 Naw-Rúz message, for example, it wrote:

> "The teaching work, both that organized by institutions of the Faith and that which is the fruit of individual initiative, must be actively carried forward so that there will be growing numbers of believers, leading more countries to the stage of entry by troops and ultimately to mass conversion." [30]

In the 1995 Riḍván message, it again spoke of the dynamics of this relationship. It pointed out that the individual believer has to take initiative in teaching and at the same time participate in the projects of the community. The Assemblies, on the other hand, are to promote individual initiative, but also create plans for collective action in which the believers can participate, putting to use their diverse talents.

> **"Fundamental to any effective response to the immediate challenges facing the community are these requisites which are especially addressed to the individual and the Local Spiritual Assembly: On the one hand is the initiative that it is the duty and privilege of the individual to take in teaching the Cause and in obtaining a deeper understanding of the purpose and requirements of the Faith. Parallel with the exercise of such initiative is the necessity of the individual's participation in collective endeavors, such as community functions and projects. On the other hand is the role of the Local Spiritual Assembly to welcome, encourage and accommodate the initiatives of individual believers to the maximum extent possible; and there is, too, the responsibility of the Assembly to devise or promote plans that will employ the talents and abilities of the individual members of its community, and that will involve individuals in collective action, such as teaching and development projects, institutes, and other group activities."** [31]

And in its 1996 Riḍván message, referring to the accomplishments of the previous year, the House of Justice stated:

> **"Systematic approaches to collective teaching activities and well-focused long-term teaching projects were fruitful and were more evident than ever before in a number of countries."** [32]

In the light of the above passages, write a few paragraphs expressing your own understanding of the need for systematic teaching campaigns designed by the institutions, and the importance of participating in them:

SECTION 26

It is not the purpose of this unit to examine how teaching campaigns should be devised, but to help you reflect on your own participation in plans and projects organized by your institutions. Nonetheless, it is necessary to pause here and mention a few words about the nature of systematic collective teaching endeavors in our communities.

Suppose for a moment that you are a member of a task force in charge of organizing a teaching campaign in an area where several communities already exist. Once your own consultations have borne fruit, your task force invites the believers of these communities to a meeting in order to present to them the project and urge them all to participate in it. The meeting is carried out in a spiritual atmosphere, a few moving talks on the importance of teaching and the role of the individual are presented, and a great deal of excitement is generated. When talks and consultations are over, one of the members of the task force summarizes the results in these words: "The campaign we are launching today is straightforward. It asks that every individual pray daily to have at least one success in teaching, that every individual mention the Faith to at least one person every day, and that every family have a fireside at least once every nineteen days."

Undoubtedly, since the task force we have imagined would have, like all Bahá'í institutions and agencies, striven to discharge its duties to the best of its ability, if the believers in the region now follow its recommendations with devotion and enthusiasm, we can assume that the communities will witness growth both in numbers and capacity, preparing them to embark on even greater undertakings. However, in order to increase our understanding of the subject, it is useful to ask whether such a plan fits at all our notion of systematic collective action. Does the plan consist of more than encouraging individuals to pursue their own personal teaching efforts, admittedly with added enthusiasm stemming from the knowledge that others are also engaged in the same kind of activity? Should not collective action be designed in such a way that the talents of individuals reinforce one another, multiplying thereby their powers. Should not the united action of a group of people bring far more results than the sum of their separate individual efforts?

In general, we should not think of a teaching project as a set of activities that are carried out in a vacuum. In the vast majority of cases, to be successful, a campaign has to be aimed at a specific population and designed with its particular social and cultural reality in mind. The methods and materials used in the project are not to be determined by the likes and dislikes of the group of people who participate in it. They should be the outcome of diligent work over an extended period of time—study, consultation, experimentation, and reflection on the methods and results of action, all guided by the institutions of the Faith. It is not unreasonable to expect, for example, that in a given country, it would take one or two years to work out the details of some type of teaching campaign for a receptive population, say, the inhabitants of certain rural areas. During that time, methods and approaches would be discovered and appropriate materials developed. Once this had been achieved, a few small pilot projects would be launched; then an increasing number of teachers would be trained and the campaign extended to region after region.

With these ideas in mind, can you write below some of the activities that might be undertaken in a campaign in a region where there are, say, fifty believers ready to participate in collective action. What would they be asked to do individually, in groups, and as separate communities. What kind of inter-community activities would be carried out?

What would your task force do in order to promote and support the activities you have mentioned above?

SECTION 27

During your life as a Bahá'í, you will participate in many types of campaigns, both those designed to proclaim Bahá'u'lláh's Message and those organized to teach the Cause and confirm souls from various strata of society. It is not possible to describe all of these here, but you should at least become familiar with the type of campaign that focuses on a very receptive population and aims at enrolling relatively large numbers of believers at a reasonably quick pace. To begin exploring the nature of such campaigns, study the following extract from a message written by the Universal House of Justice:

"When the masses of mankind are awakened and enter the Faith of God, a new process is set in motion and the growth of a new civilization begins. Witness the emergence of Christianity and of Islám. These masses are the rank and file, steeped in traditions of their own, but receptive to the new Word of God, by which, when they truly respond to it, they become so influenced as to transform those who come in contact with them.

"God's standards are different from those of men. According to men's standards, the acceptance of any cause by people of distinction, of recognized fame and status, determines the value and greatness of that cause. But, in the words of Bahá'u'lláh: 'The summons and Message which We gave were never intended to reach or to benefit one land or one people only. Mankind in its entirety must firmly adhere to whatsoever hath been revealed and vouchsafed unto it.' Or again, 'He hath endowed every soul with the capacity to recognize the signs of God. How could He, otherwise, have fulfilled His testimony unto men, if ye be of them that ponder His Cause in their hearts.' In countries where teaching the masses has succeeded, the Bahá'ís have poured out their time and effort in village areas to the same extent as they had formerly done in cities and towns. The results indicate how unwise it is to solely concentrate on one section of the population. Each National Assembly therefore should so balance its resources and harmonize its efforts that the Faith of God is taught not only to those who are readily accessible but to all sections of society, however remote they may be.

"The unsophisticated people of the world—and they form the large majority of its population—have the same right to know of the Cause of God as others. When the friends are teaching the Word of God they should be careful to give the Message in the same simplicity as it is enunciated in our Teachings. In their contacts they must show genuine and divine love. The heart of an unlettered soul is extremely sensitive; any trace of prejudice on the part of the pioneer or teacher is immediately sensed.

"When teaching among the masses, the friends should be careful not to emphasize the charitable and humanitarian aspects of the Faith as a means to win recruits. Experience has shown that when facilities such as schools, dispensaries, hospitals, or even clothes and food are offered to the people being taught, many complications arise. The prime motive should always be the response of man to God's Message, and the recognition of His Messenger. Those who declare themselves as Bahá'ís should become enchanted with the beauty of the Teachings, and touched by the love of Bahá'u'lláh. The declarants need not know all the proofs, history, laws, and principles of the Faith, but in the process of declaring themselves they must, in addition to catching the spark of faith, become basically informed about the Central Figures of the Faith, as well as the existence of laws they must follow and an administration they must obey.

"After declaration, the new believers must not be left to their own devices. Through correspondence and dispatch of visitors, through conferences and training courses, these friends must be patiently strengthened and lovingly helped to develop into full Bahá'í maturity. The beloved Guardian, referring to the duties of Bahá'í Assemblies in assisting the newly declared believer, has written: '... the members of each and every Assembly should endeavor, by their patience, their love, their tact and wisdom, to nurse, subsequent to his admission, the newcomer into Bahá'í maturity, and win him over gradually to the unreserved acceptance of whatever has been ordained in the Teachings.'" [33]

1. According to the above passage, what happens when the masses of humankind are awakened and enter the Faith of God?

2. What change occurs in the masses when they truly respond to the new Word of God?

3. How does the above passage explain one of the differences between God's standards and the standards of men?

4. Is it wise to concentrate our teaching efforts only on a small section of society to which we have easy access?

5. What is the advice of the Universal House of Justice to National Assemblies on how each is to balance its resources and harmonize its efforts?

6. Is the Message of Bahá'u'lláh only for the sophisticated? Does being sophisticated in the ways of this modern world imply wisdom and true understanding?

7. What does it mean "to give the Message in the same simplicity as it is enunciated in our teachings"? Does it mean the Message should be "watered down"?

The Act of Teaching - 135

8. What should we show forth in our contacts with the great masses of humanity?

9. When teaching, should we emphasize the charitable and humanitarian aspects of the Faith as a means to win recruits? Why not?

10. What should be the prime motive of those who choose to enter the ranks of Bahá'u'lláh's followers?

11. What sentiments should those who declare themselves as Bahá'ís have for Bahá'u'lláh and His Teachings?

12. In addition to catching the spark of faith, of what should they be informed?

13. According to the passage, what should be done following the declaration of newly enrolled believers in areas of large-scale expansion?

SECTION 28

From all that has been said up to now, we can conclude that there is no such thing as one model teaching campaign to be conducted universally throughout the Bahá'í world. We also know that to be successful, campaigns should focus on specific populations. Moreover, when the population is very receptive, the aim can be to bring in large numbers at a fairly accelerated rate. But even those projects that focus on receptive populations within the great masses of humanity can take on different forms according to the characteristics of each population and the capacities of the Bahá'ís who devise and carry out the activities. Often, however, they involve intense group action: a highly organized set of activities of a group of teachers guided by a coordinator who remain in a village or town for a certain period of time and teach the Faith. It is important for you to learn a few things about the nature of such action.

Let us suppose that you are about to participate in a project carefully designed by one of the agencies of the Faith in your region. To be specific, we will assume that the project requires small groups of some five to eight teachers to stay and work together in several towns, carrying out a range of tasks aimed at the expansion and consolidation of the Faith in each locality and the surrounding villages.

A most important idea, that you would have to keep in mind throughout the campaign, is that the success of such an endeavor depends entirely on the unity of the group. No matter how well-planned the project, no matter how experienced the teachers, if there is strife and contention in the group, its efforts will yield little fruit.

Living and working closely with others is bound to lead to tension. The causes of disagreement are usually trivial and hardly ever motivated by malice. Not infrequently, tension arises because someone shows insensitivity to the feelings of another or insists on getting his or her own way. The remedy is magnanimity and the ability to rise above the petty things of life, at least for the duration of a project. 'Abdu'l-Bahá has said:

> **"Now is the time, O ye beloved of the Lord, for ardent endeavor. Struggle ye, and strive. And since the Ancient Beauty was exposed by day and night on the field of martyrdom, let us in our turn labor hard, and hear and ponder the counsels of God; let us fling away our lives, and renounce our brief and numbered days. Let us turn our eyes away from empty fantasies of this world's divergent forms, and serve instead this preeminent purpose, this grand design. Let us not, because of our own imaginings, cut down this tree that the hand of heavenly grace hath planted; let us not, with the dark clouds of our illusions, our selfish interests, blot out the glory that streameth from the Abhá Realm. Let us not be as barriers that wall out the rolling ocean of Almighty God. Let us not prevent the pure, sweet scents from the garden of the All-Glorious Beauty from blowing far and wide. Let us not, on this day of reunion, shut out the vernal downpour of blessings from on high. Let us not consent that the splendors of the Sun of Truth should ever fade and disappear. These are the admonitions of God, as set forth in His Holy Books, His Scriptures, His Tablets that tell out His counselings to the sincere.**
>
> **"The glory rest upon you, and God's mercy, and God's blessings."** [34]

The Guardian has said:

> "Fix your gaze on the mighty possibilities, the incalculable blessings, the indomitable spirit of this growing and struggling Faith of God, and do not allow the petty disputes and inevitable differences of the present to obscure your vision of the resplendent glories which the future of the Cause has in store for its steadfast and valiant supporters." [35]

Showing respect to the coordinator and listening to his or her counsels also help the group avoid disunity. Experienced coordinators do not wait for problems to grow before they act. Indeed, knowing the importance of unity, they ensure that some of the general discussions of the group focus on this vital subject, not allowing anyone to make direct or indirect accusatory remarks about any other member of the group. The memorization of passages such as the following at the beginning of the project brings marvelous results:

> "If any differences arise amongst you, behold Me standing before your face, and overlook the faults of one another for My name's sake and as a token of your love for My manifest and resplendent Cause. We love to see you at all times consorting in amity and concord within the paradise of My good-pleasure, and to inhale from your acts the fragrance of friendliness and unity, of loving-kindness and fellowship. Thus counseleth you the All-Knowing, the Faithful. We shall always be with you; if We inhale the perfume of your fellowship, Our heart will assuredly rejoice, for naught else can satisfy Us. To this beareth witness every man of true understanding." [36]

An experienced coordinator also knows that unity is easier to maintain when everyone is aware of the significance of the work to be done and the sublimity of the goals to be achieved. When such an understanding exists, people have less difficulty putting aside their own interests and selflessly give their all to the tasks at hand. Pause for a moment and think: Would you be willing to harm a campaign which is destined to bring the joy of recognizing Bahá'u'lláh to scores of waiting souls for any one of the following?

_____ Because you want to listen to your favorite music during the campaign every day?

_____ Because you do not like the food that is being served?

_____ Because you like to sleep late in the morning?

_____ Because you cherish your privacy above all things?

_____ Because you feel that your favorite teaching method should be adopted by the group?

SECTION 29

Another idea to be mentioned is that such intensive campaigns are not occasions for rest and relaxation. They require long hours of hard yet joyful work.

There is a mistaken notion in the world of what constitutes fun. Some people act as if the very purpose of life were to have fun, and fun they define only in terms of trivial pastimes. But how can such "fun" be compared with the real joy of sharing the Message of Bahá'u'lláh with others, of seeing them uplifted by the spirit of faith, of witnessing firsthand the spiritual and numerical growth of the Bahá'í community. If ever in a campaign the desire for comfort and self-indulgence grows strong, it can be overcome by the remembrance of 'Abdu'l-Bahá, the perfect Exemplar, and His tireless efforts to propagate the Cause. Here are some of His words:

> **"Follow in the footsteps of 'Abdu'l-Bahá, and in the pathway of the Abhá Beauty, long at every moment to give up your lives. Shine out like the daystar, be unresting as the sea; even as the clouds of heaven, shed ye life upon field and hill, and like unto April winds, blow freshness through those human trees, and bring them to their blossoming."** [37]

> **"That is to say, man must become evanescent in God. Must forget his own selfish conditions that he may thus arise to the station of sacrifice. It should be to such a degree that if he sleep, it should not be for pleasure, but to rest the body in order to do better, to speak better, to explain more beautifully, to serve the servants of God and to prove the truths. When he remains awake, he should seek to be attentive, serve the Cause of God and sacrifice his own stations for those of God. When he attains to this station, the confirmations of the Holy Spirit will surely reach him, and man with this power can withstand all who inhabit the earth."** [38]

> **"I hope, from the bounties of the Exalted, the Quickener of the souls, that thou mayest not rest for one moment but pulsate constantly like unto the pulsation of an artery in the body of the world, to infuse the spirit of life in the souls and suffer the people to soar up to the zenith of the Kingdom."** [39]

> **"These shall labor ceaselessly, by day and by night, shall heed neither trials nor woe, shall suffer no respite in their efforts, shall seek no repose, shall disregard all ease and comfort, and, detached and unsullied, shall consecrate every fleeting moment of their lives to the diffusion of the divine fragrance and the exaltation of God's holy Word. Their faces will radiate heavenly gladness, and their hearts be filled with joy. Their souls will be inspired, and their foundation stand secure. They shall scatter in the world, and travel throughout all regions. They shall raise their voices in every assembly, and adorn and revive every gathering. They shall speak in every tongue, and interpret every hidden meaning. They shall reveal the mysteries of the Kingdom, and manifest unto everyone the signs of God. They shall burn brightly even as a candle in the heart of every assembly, and beam forth as a star upon every horizon. The gentle breezes wafted from the garden of their hearts shall perfume and revive the souls of men, and the revelations of their minds, even as showers, will reinvigorate the peoples and nations of the world."** [40]

SECTION 30

Yet another idea that is important to bear in mind when participating in an intensive teaching campaign relates to respect for other people's customs. Some of the projects in which you will take part will focus on populations whose customs are similar to your own. But it is to be expected that you will also have the opportunity to teach among people of other cultural backgrounds. In these cases, it is essential that you appreciate the culture of the population you are serving and show genuine respect towards it.

The subject of culture is a complex one, and this is not the place to enter into an in-depth analysis of it. Yet, for the purposes of this unit, two points need to be brought to your attention.

The first concerns how one responds to the various elements of a culture. Every culture in the world contains elements that are praiseworthy, and elements that would best be discarded. And then there are aspects of all cultures that are neither good nor bad; they simply represent the diversity of ways that things can be viewed, understood, expressed and done. For a Bahá'í, the standard of what is correct and what is undesirable is, of course, Bahá'u'lláh's Revelation. For example, that a certain people regards women as inferior to men cannot be considered acceptable by a Bahá'í in the name of culture. This is an aspect of that specific culture that would have to change as it becomes illumined with the light of the Teachings. On the other hand, if a culture places strong emphasis on fostering cooperation and a sense of community, then this is to be appreciated and cherished.

In general, it is not difficult to identify those elements of a culture that are either in clear agreement with the Teachings of the Faith or in direct conflict with them. But cultural issues become more complicated when the elements in question do not easily fall into one or the other category. Consider, for example, the diversity of music that exists in the world. We know from the Writings that music is to be uplifting to the human spirit. Clearly songs that arouse desires of the lower nature are not acceptable, and the participants of a teaching campaign would surely not engage in listening to them. But apart from these, numerous types of music have flourished in the varied cultures of the world, and often people are attached to their own. In this case, then, the obvious norm is for you to be respectful of the likes and dislikes of those among whom you are teaching. The purpose of the campaign is to bring to them the Message of Bahá'u'lláh; you are not there to impose on them your own tastes.

One special element of every culture is its perception of what is polite and courteous. When the subtleties of politeness are not understood, it is easy to offend a people or even, unknowingly, hurt them. Humor, which is closely related to courtesy, is another area of great sensitivity. There is one maxim regarding humor that, if followed, saves a great deal of pain and embarrassment: Reject all jokes that in one way or another belittle a people of some ethnicity, race or nationality, and banish from your comments any statement that implies in the least inequality or conflict between men and women. There is nothing funny about jokes and remarks of this kind; they are at best remnants from humanity's childhood that should be thrown away.

The second point you will need to bear in mind when working among another people is that, if approached with proper attitudes, the interaction between diverse cultures is actually an enjoyable experience. We all like to hear music from other parts and learn about unfamiliar customs and traditions. Through interaction, the cultures of living peoples change; they are not things of museums to be preserved and visited by curious observers.

The interaction of cultures, then, is a phenomenon that will occur naturally. The problem arises when one group considers its culture so superior that it decides to aggressively propagate it and erase all others. When teaching among a population whose culture is different from our own, we have to be aware of this danger and recognize the fact that every people can move directly to Bahá'u'lláh; they do not first need to adopt our culture. The following ideas may help you in this respect.

The diverse peoples of the world may be seen as points scattered on the outer surface of a sphere with Bahá'u'lláh at its center, at its core. There are forces in the world that are trying to pull all the points towards one pole, bringing them together in what is claimed to be a universal culture. But, when this happens, the points only move from one place on the surface of the sphere to another, and their distance from the center, their distance from Bahá'u'lláh, does not change. On the other hand, if each one of these points, if each one of these peoples, is allowed to move along its own direct path towards Bahá'u'lláh, they will naturally come closer to one another. Their cultures will change and be enriched as they each make contributions to the emergence of a world civilization.

SECTION 31

One way to examine the characteristics of the kind of teaching campaign we are considering here is to divide it into several blocks of time, each dedicated to a particular set of activities. During each period, the participants in the project follow, with the help of the coordinator, certain procedures established by the institutions in charge of the project. These procedures do not necessarily represent the only way of doing things, but a mature participant knows how to forgo his or her own tastes and habits in order to allow for the sound dynamics of group action to develop.

The first block of time is made up of the early morning hours. Generally, people can go to sleep at night and wake up in the morning when it is convenient for them. However, most coordinators require the participants to begin the work of the group early in the morning, for experience has shown that this adds a great deal to the effectiveness of the day. For one thing, the vast majority of the people of the world, among whom this type of campaign is usually conducted, are early risers.

The first hour or so of the day is, of course, a personal time. And the respect and consideration that the members of the group show one another during this period shape to a large extent how they will interact throughout the day. Apart from the time spent washing, dressing and tidying one's personal belongings, these couple of hours constitute a most intimate moment for each person to turn to God and commune with Him. This is the time to reflect within one's own heart on the bounties that one is continually receiving from God, and prepare oneself to receive the day's portion of these infinite bestowals. This is the time to retire to a corner and engage in prayer and meditation, beseeching with intense ardor that one's efforts, small as they may be, are accepted at His Holy Threshold and blessed with divine confirmations. How precious is the remembrance of the passages recited in those early hours of the morning:

> "O Lord! I am a broken-winged bird and desire to soar in Thy limitless space. How is it possible for me to do this save through Thy providence and grace, Thy confirmation and assistance." [41]

> "I beseech Thee, by Him Who is the Fountainhead of Thy Revelation and the Dayspring of Thy signs, to make my heart to be a receptacle of Thy love and of remembrance of Thee. Knit it, then, to Thy most great Ocean, that from it may flow out the living waters of Thy wisdom and the crystal streams of Thy glorification and praise." [42]

> "I beg of Thee, O Thou King of existence and Protector of the seen and the unseen, to make whosoever arises to serve Thy Cause as a sea moving by Thy desire, as one ablaze with the fire of Thy Sacred Tree, shining from the horizon of the heaven of Thy will." [43]

> "O my God, aid Thou Thy servant to raise up the Word, and to refute what is vain and false, to establish the truth, to spread the sacred verses abroad, reveal the splendors, and make the morning's light to dawn in the hearts of the righteous." [44]

> "O God! O God! Thou seest my weakness, lowliness and humility before Thy creatures; nevertheless, I have trusted in Thee and have arisen in the promotion of Thy teachings among Thy strong servants, relying on Thy power and might." [45]

> "O my God! O my God! Thou seest me in my lowliness and weakness, occupied with the greatest undertaking, determined to raise Thy word among the masses and to spread Thy teachings among Thy peoples. How can I succeed unless Thou assist me with the breath of the Holy Spirit, help me to triumph by the hosts of Thy glorious kingdom, and shower upon me Thy confirmations, which alone can change a gnat into an eagle, a drop of water into rivers and seas, and an atom into lights and suns?" [46]

> "O Lord! I am weak, strengthen me with Thy power and potency. My tongue falters, suffer me to utter Thy commemoration and praise. I am lowly, honor me through admitting me into Thy kingdom. I am remote, cause me to approach the threshold of Thy mercifulness." [47]

> "O Lord! Should the breath of the Holy Spirit confirm the weakest of creatures, he would attain all to which he aspireth and would possess anything he desireth." [48]

> "O Lord! Make manifest in Thy lands humble and submissive souls, their faces illumined with the rays of guidance, severed from the world, extolling Thy Name, uttering Thy praise, and diffusing the fragrance of Thy holiness amongst mankind." [49]

"O God, my God! Aid Thou Thy trusted servants to have loving and tender hearts. Help them to spread, amongst all the nations of the earth, the light of guidance that cometh from the Company on high." [50]

"Verily, Thy lovers thirst, O my Lord; lead them to the wellspring of bounty and grace. Verily, they hunger; send down unto them Thy heavenly table. Verily, they are naked; robe them in the garments of learning and knowledge." [51]

"O Thou incomparable God! O Thou Lord of the Kingdom! These souls are Thy heavenly army. Assist them and, with the cohorts of the Supreme Concourse, make them victorious, so that each one of them may become like unto a regiment and conquer these countries through the love of God and the illumination of divine teachings." [52]

In addition to allowing the individual participants time for prayer and mediation, the coordinator organizes a prayer session for the entire group during this period. And, naturally, some of the members have the duty to prepare the food and serve the first meal of the day. This is a task to be accepted wholeheartedly and carried out graciously by each member, for the love of God has to be translated into service to His loved ones; small acts of loving-kindness are endowed with immense potency and are able to energize a group of dedicated souls determined to work together in unity.

SECTION 32

The second block of time is dedicated to the deepening of the group itself. This is an important activity and neglecting it would diminish the effectiveness of the campaign. The teacher must be in tune with the spiritual forces that bring about the transformation of souls. And to achieve this, it is essential that the teacher's mind and heart resonate with the power of the Word of God. An experienced coordinator is ever ready to bring to the attention of the group specific passages from the writings that speak to themes relevant to the work of the day. The memorization of such passages is indeed like heavenly food that nourishes the participants and maintains the spiritual atmosphere of the campaign. As an exercise, you may wish to look for some passages that would be appropriate for the deepening of a group in an intensive teaching project.

SECTION 33

The third block of time is dedicated to the activities of the campaign per se. These, as we have repeatedly said, vary according to the nature of each project. In all campaigns, however, this period is one of constant, focused and resolute action. Usually, at the end of the deepening session, the group will have consulted with the help of the coordinator on the tasks and challenges of the day. This is the time, then, for every member of the group to call on the powers of divine assistance and devote every thought and action to bringing Bahá'u'lláh's life-giving Message to waiting souls.

Here it must be remembered that the purpose of such teaching projects is never the mere enrollment of large numbers. There are several related activities that have to be undertaken: Receptive individuals have to be sought. They then have to be engaged in meaningful conversation and helped to recognize Bahá'u'lláh as the Manifestation of God for today and enter into the stronghold of His Covenant. Newly enrolled believers, as well as the other Bahá'ís of the locality, have to be called on at their homes and a series of deepening themes shared with them. Every effort must be made to create in the members of the Bahá'í community the necessary zeal for teaching and to integrate them into the activities of the campaign. Often special attention has to be given to children by offering them moral education classes daily. Moreover, people in leadership positions in the locality should be visited and familiarized with the aims and purposes of the Faith.

The actual methods of teaching can take on various levels of formality. For instance, it can be left entirely to each individual teacher to determine how he or she will go about meeting people, introducing the Faith to them and explaining to them its fundamental verities. But, it is also possible for a campaign to follow a more formal program. To give you an example, the organizers of one campaign have adopted a very formal approach of registering people in a series of classes of a few hours each conducted over five consecutive days. The themes they have chosen for the classes are: human nature and the life of the soul for day 1, the power of prayer for day 2, God and His Manifestations for day 3, the Covenant of Bahá'u'lláh for day 4, the Bahá'í community for day 5. On the sixth day a Unity Feast is held. By this time, many of those attending the classes will have been moved to declare their faith in Bahá'u'lláh and will have become members of the Bahá'í community.

Although the activities of this period have to be carried out with a sense of urgency and with dispatch, we should remember that the teaching of receptive souls cannot be hasty and superficial. Even when individuals accept the Faith quickly, they are in need of a number of visits during the campaign until a strong foundation for their future development as Bahá'ís is built. A secret that every experienced teacher has learned in this respect is that believers, newly enrolled and veteran alike, are greatly confirmed when they participate in the teaching of friends or family members, initially with the help of the visiting teachers and then gradually by themselves. It proves most effective to ask those who accept the Faith for the names of the other members of their family who may wish to receive the glad-tidings of the Promised One of all Ages and arrange to meet these family members together.

SECTION 34

The final block of time is made of the evening hours. Every experienced coordinator knows that evenings in a campaign are productive periods and should be fully exploited. Sometimes large gatherings open to the entire village or town are held during this time. In these gatherings, well-prepared talks are delivered, and musical performances, skits, and dramatic presentations are given. A concerted effort is made to create a sense of community and generate enthusiasm. In other instances, the same is achieved through various smaller meetings and formal classes.

It is important for the participants in the campaign to realize that they should take active part in the evening activities. This is not the time for them to relax or to socialize among themselves. They have to be alert and hospitable, making sure that every person present in a meeting, large or small, feels welcome, that each one receives attention, and that everyone's questions are answered.

With such gatherings, the work of the day comes to an end. But, before the participants retire, there is one more activity to which they must attend. A final meeting is needed for the group itself to discuss the experience of the day. We must remember that consistent success in teaching depends on the extent to which we approach it with an attitude of learning. The discussions of this last meeting, then, should be kept free from both false humility and boastfulness. The task is to express the lessons learned during the day with humble gratitude.

SECTION 35

This short description of one type of campaign, often held among highly receptive populations, concludes our exploration of the act of teaching, both as a personal initiative and as a collective endeavor. In thinking about the two, you must realize that the spiritual principles that come into play are the same in both. Yet the process of enrolling a few friends into the Bahá'í community is different from that of bringing thousands and thousands of the inhabitants of a region into the Faith. A simple analogy will help to clarify this point. The principles governing the growth of plants are the same in a small flower bed and in a farm spread over hundreds of hectares. Yet tending a few plants in one's personal garden is very different from farming large extensions.

When you have a few friends who have enrolled in the Faith, you will continue to nurture each one of them as part of your own personal teaching plan, spending time with them and deepening them until they become ardent supporters of the Faith and active in promoting the Cause. So, too, when the institutions organize a campaign among a receptive population, a large percentage of which will readily accept Bahá'u'lláh if His Message is presented clearly and with zeal, plans need to be laid to deepen the newly enrolled believers. But, here, it is no longer possible for a few teachers to deepen the hundreds they have helped to bring into the Faith, and capable believers from among the population itself have to be trained in order to carry out this and the many other tasks associated with rapidly expanding communities. At the heart of such plans, then, is the training institute. On this subject the Universal House of Justice has said:

> **"With the growth in the number of enrollments, it has become apparent that such occasional courses of instruction and the informal activities of community life, though important, are not sufficient as a means of human resource development, for they have resulted in only a relatively small band of active supporters of the Cause. These believers, no matter how dedicated, no matter how willing to make sacrifices, cannot attend to the needs of hundreds, much less thousands, of fledgling local communities. Systematic attention has to be given by Bahá'í institutions to training a significant number of believers and assisting them in serving the Cause according to their God-given talents and capacities.**

"The development of human resources on a large scale requires that the establishment of institutes be viewed in a new light. In many regions, it has become imperative to create institutes as organizational structures dedicated to systematic training. The purpose of such training is to endow ever-growing contingents of believers with the spiritual insights, the knowledge, and the skills needed to carry out the many tasks of accelerated expansion and consolidation, including the teaching and deepening of a large number of people—adults, youth and children. This purpose can best be achieved through well-organized, formal programs consisting of courses that follow appropriately designed curricula." [53]

Clearly, then, participating in institute courses, whether as a student or as a teacher, is of vital importance. In a message written to the believers in Latin America and the Caribbean, the House of Justice has said:

"Plans focusing on these areas of large-scale expansion will necessarily seek to mobilize an appreciable number of believers within each population not only to labor diligently in their own local communities, but also to serve as long- and short-term pioneers and visiting teachers in other localities. Training programs, with which many of your communities have considerable experience, constitute a most potent instrument for the accomplishment of such a vast mobilization. We call upon you, then, to support the work of the training institutes in your countries, the more experienced among you giving generously of their time as teachers so that courses can be offered widely and consistently. As you acquire new knowledge and skills through these programs, you will be able to put into practice with enthusiasm and zeal what you have learned, and arise to shoulder the manifold responsibilities that accelerated expansion and consolidation demand." [54]

It must be a source of great joy to you to know that by participating in the courses of your institute, you are responding to the call of the Universal House of Justice. You will be equally glad to know that the next book of the Ruhi Institute is designed for the training of tutors of the first six books. When you study it, you will increase your capacity to maintain study circles not only in your own town or village but in neighboring ones as well. But, for now, your immediate task is to put into practice what you have learned in this book, by volunteering to participate in a national, regional or local campaign and by implementing your personal teaching plan.

REFERENCES

1. From the 1974 Naw-Rúz message of the Universal House of Justice, published in *Teaching the Bahá'í Faith: Compilations and a Statement Prepared by the Research Department of the Universal House of Justice* (Mona Vale: Bahá'í Publications Australia, 1995), no. 312, p. 160.

2. Shoghi Effendi, *The Advent of Divine Justice* (Wilmette: Bahá'í Publishing Trust, 1990), p. 48.

3. Bahá'u'lláh, *The Kitáb-i-Aqdas: The Most Holy Book* (Wilmette: Bahá'í Publishing Trust, 1993), p. 22.

4. *The Universal House of Justice,* Wellspring of Guidance: Messages 1963-1968 (Wilmette: Bahá'í Publishing Trust, 1976), p. 32.

5. *Gleanings from the Writings of Bahá'u'lláh* (Wilmette: Bahá'í Publishing Trust, 1983), CXX, p. 255.

6. Bahá'u'lláh, *The Hidden Words* (Wilmette: Bahá'í Publishing Trust, 1990), Arabic no. 4, p. 4.

7. *Gleanings from the Writings of Bahá'u'lláh*, IV, p. 6.

8. *Bhagavad Gita 4:7-8.*

9. Paris Talks: Addresses given by 'Abdu'l-Bahá in Paris in 1911-1912 (London: Bahá'í Publishing Trust, 1995), p. 46.

10. *Bahá'u'lláh, Bahá'í Prayers: A Selection of Prayers Revealed by Bahá'u'lláh, the Báb, and 'Abdu'l-Bahá* (Wilmette: Bahá'í Publishing Trust, 1993). p. 211.

11. *Gleanings from the Writings of Bahá'u'lláh*, XLV, pp. 99-100.

12. The Báb, *Bahá'í Prayers*, p. 28.

13. Ibid., p. 29.

14. Bahá'u'lláh, *The Kitáb-i-Aqdas: The Most Holy Book* (Wilmette: Bahá'í Publishing Trust, 1993), p. 22.

15. Bahá'u'lláh, *Bahá'í Prayers*, p. 4.

16. *The Hidden Words*, Persian no. 44, p. 37.

17. Ibid., Arabic no. 13, pp. 6-7.

18. *Tablets of Abdu'l-Baha Abbas* (Chicago: Bahá'í Publishing Committee, 1930), vol. 3, pp. 579-80.

19. 'Abdu'l-Bahá, *Bahá'í Prayers*, p. 152.

20. *Gleanings from the Writings of Bahá'u'lláh*, CXXIX, pp. 279-80.

21. Shoghi Effendi, *The Advent of Divine Justice*, p. 51.

22. Ibid., p. 51.

23. Ibid., pp. 51-52.

24. Ibid., p. 52.

25. Ibid., p. 52.

26. Ibid., p. 52.

27. Shoghi Effendi, *Messages to America: Selected Letters and Cablegrams Addressed to the Bahá'ís of North America, 1932-1946* (Wilmette: Bahá'í Publishing Committee, 1947), pp. 5-6.

28. Ibid., p. 7.

29. Ibid., p. 79.

30. From the 1979 Naw-Rúz message written by the Universal House of Justice to the Bahá'ís of the world, published in *Promoting Entry by Troops* (Riviera Beach: Palabra Publications, 1996), no. 32, p. 34.

31. From the 1995 Riḍván message written by the Universal House of Justice to the Bahá'ís of the world.

32. From the 1996 Riḍván message to the Bahá'ís of the world, published in *The Four Year Plan: Messages of the Universal House of Justice* (Riviera Beach: Palabra Publications, 1996), p. 25.

33. The Universal House of Justice, Wellspring of Guidance, pp. 31-33.

34. *Selections from the Writings of 'Abdu'l-Bahá* (Wilmette: Bahá'í Publishing Trust, 1997), no. 207, pp. 275-76.

35. Postscript in the handwriting of Shoghi Effendi appended to an unpublished letter dated 9 May 1933 written on his behalf to an individual believer.

36. *Gleanings from the Writings of Bahá'u'lláh*, CXLVI, pp. 315-16.

37. *Selections from the Writings of 'Abdu'l-Bahá*, no. 200, p. 257.

38. *Tablets of Abdu'l-Baha Abbas* (Chicago: Bahá'í Publishing Committee, 1930), vol. 2, p. 460.

39. *Tablets of Abdu'l-Baha Abbas*, vol. 3, p. 727.

40. *Selections from the Writings of 'Abdu'l-Bahá*, no. 204, p. 263.

41. 'Abdu'l-Bahá, *Bahá'í Prayers*, pp. 179-80.

42. Bahá'u'lláh, *Bahá'í Prayers*, pp. 170-71.

43. Ibid., p. 172.

44. 'Abdu'l-Bahá, *Bahá'í Prayers*, p. 174.

45. Ibid., p. 179.

46. Ibid., p. 186.

47. Ibid., p. 187.

48. Ibid., p. 180.

49. Ibid., p. 182.

50. Ibid., pp. 174-75.

51. Ibid., pp. 175-76.

52. Ibid., p. 177.

53. From a message dated 26 December 1995 written by the Universal House of Justice to the Conference of the Continental Boards of Counselors, published in *The Four Year Plan*, p. 7.

54. From the 1996 Riḍván message written by the Universal House of Justice to the followers of Bahá'u'lláh in Latin America and the Caribbean, published in *The Four Year Plan, pp. 62-63.*